UNITED STATES TANKS AND TANK DESTROYERS OF THE SECOND WORLD WAR

UNITED STATES TANKS AND TANK DESTROYERS OF THE SECOND WORLD WAR

MICHAEL GREEN

Pen & Sword
MILITARY

First published in Great Britain in 2021 by
PEN & SWORD MILITARY
an imprint of
Pen & Sword Books Ltd
47 Church Street
Barnsley
South Yorkshire
S70 2AS

ISBN 978-1-52678-747-7

Typeset by Concept, Huddersfield, West Yorkshire HD4 5JL.
Printed and bound the UK by CPI Group (UK) Ltd, Croydon, CR0 4YY.

Pen & Sword Books Limited incorporates the imprints of Atlas, Archaeology, Aviation,
Discovery, Family History, Fiction, History, Maritime, Military, Military Classics,
Politics, Select, Transport, True Crime, Air World, Frontline Publishing, Leo Cooper,
Remember When, Seaforth Publishing, The Praetorian Press, Wharncliffe Local History,
Wharncliffe Transport, Wharncliffe True Crime and White Owl.

For a complete list of Pen & Sword titles please contact
PEN & SWORD BOOKS LIMITED
47 Church Street, Barnsley, South Yorkshire S70 2AS, England
E-mail: enquiries@pen-and-sword.co.uk
Website: www.pen-and-sword.co.uk

Contents

Dedication

The author dedicates this book to Medal of Honor recipient, Gunnery Sergeant Robert H. McCard, US Marine Corps. His citation reads:

> For conspicuous gallantry and intrepidity at the risk of his life above and beyond the call of duty while serving as Platoon Sergeant of Company A, Fourth Tank Battalion, Fourth Marine Division, during the battle for enemy Japanese-held Saipan, Mariana Islands, on June 16, 1944. Cut off from the other units of his platoon when his tank was put out of action by a battery of enemy 77mm guns, Gunnery Sergeant McCard carried on resolutely, bringing all the tank's weapons to bear on the enemy, until the severity of hostile fire caused him to order his crew out the escape hatch while he courageously exposed himself to enemy guns by hurling hand grenades, in order to cover the evacuation of his men. Seriously wounded during this action and with his supply of grenades exhausted, Gunnery Sergeant McCard dismantled one of the tank's machine guns and faced the Japanese for the second time to deliver vigorous fire into positions, destroying sixteen of the enemy but sacrificing himself to ensure the safety of his crew. His valiant fighting spirit and supreme loyalty in the face of almost certain death reflect the highest credit upon Gunnery Sergeant McCard and the United States Naval Service. He gallantly gave his life for his country.

Foreword

The latest book by Michael Green takes the reader through the whirlwind, breakneck-speed race to build light, medium and heavy tanks and tank destroyers not only for the US Military, but to Lend-Lease supply our allies.

The author, with his expertise on writing about the weapons systems of the Second World War and using the official US Center of Military History 'Green Series' along with associated historical pamphlets, official reports and autobiographies, lays out a comprehensive narrative broken into six chapters. Each chapter is chock full of information, the trials and tribulations of development and fielding of weapons systems. Each system receives a thorough treatment of armament, protective armor, barrel design, weapons and many other characteristics that are carried forward to the next design or discarded altogether.

It is easy to get lost in the many letter designations of organizations involved in vehicle production, those in Washington DC and later in Detroit. The author, instead of trying to maneuver through the political and turf issues generated in the nation's capital, relies on specific organizations, personalities and programs that specifically affected tank production. While the list is not comprehensive, it does give the reader the flavor of the difficulties faced in vehicle production. Additionally, there were two reorganizations within the Army that would centralize contracting, vehicle design and production to the Tank-Automotive Center (T-AC) in Detroit.

Imagine if you will just one tank: the number of parts and components and sub-systems that make up the tank. Within that number of parts, let's say 14,000 parts, are major contractors, subcontractors, delivery schedules, production, tool and dye work, lathe and polishing of metal parts. With each single piece of material or sub-component is a contract between the Army and the main contractor, who would sub-contract out parts and do their own contracts with these companies. Now take the bit described above and multiply it by hundreds of thousands for Ordnance equipment, to the tune of more than 3 trillion in today's dollars; 50 percent alone was contracted by the Office, Chief of Ordnance Detroit! The numbers are staggering, and so was the job ahead for the Army.

This is where the author deftly weaves his narrative through the confusing and sometimes contradictory organizational structures and brings the focus onto vehicle systems. The strong point of this text is how the author places the reader in the driver's seat, of vehicle decisions made, trade-offs, experiments and what can only be described as the 'iron triangle' of vehicle development that is with us today: the choices between survivability, reliability and maneuverability imposed on the power, performance and protection triangle.

The text is clearly written and crisp, with many highlights and surprises throughout the chapters, including added inserts of concise information on particular subjects. Discussions on armor, engines and tracks give military vehicle restoration enthusiasts, historians and modelers information on a wide variety of vehicles. Once again, the author's latest work significantly adds to the historiography of the Second World War and vehicle development.

Randy R. Talbot
Command Historian (Retired)
US Army Tank-automotive and Armaments
Command (TACOM)

Acknowledgements

The historical images in this work come from the files of the National Archives, the US Army's Tank and Automotive Command (TACOM) and various US Army museums. For the sake of brevity, the image credits for pictures from the files of the former Patton Museum of Cavalry and Armor are shortened to just the Patton Museum.

Contemporary pictures came from many friends that are named in the image credits, especially Pierre-Olivier Buan, whose countless photographs grace this book and many others by the author.

As with all published works, authors depend on many friends for assistance in reviewing their work. A special word of thanks goes to Sherman tank researcher/historian Joe DeMarco for his assistance with this book and others by the author. Others that contributed their thoughts include Peter Shyvers, Ted Dannemiller, Joshua Collins and Eric Albertson.

A wonderful source of more detailed and extremely accurate information on Sherman tanks can be found on the Sherman Minutia website hosted by Pierre-Olivier Buan, Joe DeMarco and Liefe Hulbert.

The author would also like to thank the historians and staff at WW2 Armor for their support and assistance (please visit them and follow their efforts at ww2armor.org).

Notes to the Reader

1. Due to the book's size and format, this work is only a very broad overview of the history of American tanks and tank destroyers.
2. Vehicle weights are in their fully-loaded configuration and listed in American short tons.
3. Vehicle production numbers are taken from the *Procurement* supplement to the US Army in the Second World War 'Green Series'.

Chapter One

Light Tanks

Upon the beginning of the Second World War on September 1, 1939, the most numerous light tank model in the US Army's inventory was the four-man M2 series. The initial production version was the 9.5-ton M2A2, with the government-owned Rock Island Arsenal building 237 examples (some sources state 239) in fiscal year 1937 (July 1, 1936 through June 30, 1937).

A series of improvements to the M2A2 led to the modified and heavier 10.5-ton version designated the M2A3. Seventy-two (or possibly seventy-three) came out of the government-owned and operated Rock Island Arsenal in the next fiscal year.

The turret-mounted armament on both the M2A2 and M2A3 consisted of two machine guns. One was a .50 caliber machine gun, then considered an anti-tank weapon. The second was a Browning .30 caliber machine gun, the anti-personnel weapon. Both vehicles had an additional .30 caliber machine gun mounted in the front hull.

Combat Cars

Under the terms of the (US) National Defense Act of 1920, only the US Army's Infantry Branch could procure and operate tanks. The US Army's Cavalry Branch needed the cross-country speed and mobility of a tracked vehicle too, but technically could not have tanks. Therefore a subterfuge was employed: their versions of light tanks were known as 'Combat Cars' which included the 9.5-ton M1 and 12.5-ton M2 (the latter an improved version of the former). Eighty-nine or ninety examples of the M1 and thirty-four of the M2 left the construction line between 1937 and 1940.

Differences

Whereas the Infantry Branch's light tanks had two separate one-man machine-gun-armed turrets, the Cavalry Branch's combat cars had a single two-man turret, armed with two machine guns.

Due to interwar funding constraints, the cavalry's combat cars shared the same chassis and suspension systems as the infantry's light tanks M2A2 and M2A3. Those funding limitations reflected the American public's interwar isolationist beliefs and the economic effects of the Great Depression (1929–33).

The Armored Force

With the formation of the separate 'Armored Force' on July 10, 1940, considered a service test rather than a new branch of the US Army, all tanks and combat cars came under its control. The service test label was chosen to appease the branch chiefs of the artillery, infantry and cavalry, who felt threatened by another branch acquiring too much clout and siphoning off funding.

On August 22, 1940 the label 'Combat Car' disappeared, with all now referred to as light tanks by the Armored Force. The M1 Combat Car became the Light Tank M1A1 and the M2 Combat Car became the Light Tank M1A2. Neither the M2A2, M2A3 nor the re-designated combat cars would see front-line service in the Second World War. Instead they saw use as training vehicles in the United States.

On July 2, 1943 the Armored Force became the 'Armored Command', and in turn the 'Armored Center' on February 19, 1944. The name changes reflected the waning of its bureaucratic clout as the Army Ground Forces (AGF), under the command of Lieutenant General Lesly J. McNair, took over defining doctrine and overseeing tank development; the latter role was shared with the Ordnance Department.

The Place of the Light Tank

The organization of the Armored Force came about in response to German tank-led military success in Poland, France and the Low Countries during 1939 and the early summer of 1940. It reflected the Army's rethink on how it needed to be organized to battle German military ground forces in the future.

Indicating the importance of light tanks to the Army in 1940, its first armored division Table of Organization and Equipment (TO&E) called for 287 light tanks and only 120 medium tanks. These tanks found themselves divided between six light tank battalions and two medium tank battalions.

On 1 March 1942 the Army came up with a new armored division TO&E calling for 158 light tanks and 232 medium tanks. The tanks were formed into two regiments, with each having two battalions of medium tanks and one of the light tanks. Even though there were now fewer light tanks in the armored divisions, light tanks were still considered the offensive spearhead of the division, with the medium tanks in a supporting role.

M2A4 Light Tank

The Spanish Civil War (July 1936 to April 1939), and the combat lessons distilled from that conflict, led some in the US Army to rethink what they wanted to see in further light tank designs. Better armament and thicker frontal armor (proof against 37mm anti-tank rounds) were at the top of the list. This resulted in development work on another light tank, standardized in December 1938 as the M2A4.

Production of the four-man M2A4 did not begin until May 1940 and ended in April 1942, with 375 examples built. Because the Rock Island Arsenal could not construct as many M2A4s as the US Army required, contracts were given to American Car and Foundry, the first time in twenty years that tank construction was awarded to a commercial firm.

From the US Army official history series of the Second World War, in the volume titled *The Ordnance Department: Procurement and Supply* is the following extract: 'American Car and Foundry Company (ACF) engineers immediately set to work checking more than 2,000 blueprints and placing orders for parts and materials. The 12-ton M2A4 required more than 2,800 different parts, totaling over 14,000 individual pieces – not counting engines or accessories.'

M2A4 Armament

A progressively upgraded version of the M2A3, the M2A4 had a single two-man turret, with its main armament, a 37mm gun. It had a slightly shorter-barreled version of the 37mm towed anti-tank gun just introduced into service with the US Army Infantry Branch. From the Ordnance Standard Catalog of 1944 is a description of the 37mm guns installed in early American light tanks:

> The 37mm tank guns were developed from the 37mm Anti-tank Gun M3, the first model being the 37mm Tank Gun M5. Addition of an automatically opened breechblock changed the designation to the M6 ... The gun may be elevated by a hand-wheel, but a throw-out lever permits free movement of the gun ... A spent-case deflector is bolted to the recoil cylinder and has suspended from it a bag to receive cartridge cases.

> **Face Hardened Armor**
>
> Face Hardened Armor (FHA) is a standard steel armor plate which has been put through an extra heating process to harden its outer surface, while retaining the ductility of the original armor plate. Ductility is the property that allows a material to withstand large amounts of deformation before fracturing.
>
> The FHA plates' metallurgical content made welding very difficult, so to save time and expense the plates were bolted or riveted together. The result was early tanks that were both lightly armored and had box-like shapes that were more prone to penetration by over-matching projectiles. Not until 1941 did American industry master the skill of welding FHA plates together.
>
> Eventually, FHA plates for building tanks fell out of favor with American industry for several reasons. These included the fact that it was hard to make and difficult to machine. With a large number of tanks to be built for the US Army and Lend-Lease orders, the making of sufficient FHA plates would have proven impossible within the existing limitations of both manpower and machine tools.

In addition to a coaxial .30 caliber machine gun fitted alongside the turret-mounted 37mm main gun, the M2A4 had a ball mount .30 caliber machine gun in the lower front hull plate and a fixed, forward-firing .30 caliber machine gun in each of the tank's upper hull sponsons over the tracks. Tank upper hulls were also known as 'superstructures'.

M2A4 Armor Protection

Compared to the thickest frontal armor of 22mm (0.87in) on the M2A3, the thickest frontal armor on the M2A4 rose to 25mm (1in). The combination of the 37mm gun and thicker frontal armor increased the M2A4's weight to almost 13 tons. All the light tanks in the M2 series featured face-hardened armor (FHA), as had the cavalry's combat cars.

Despite the increase in its frontal armor, the M2A4 remained vulnerable to 37mm anti-tank fire. To have made the tank's frontal armor impervious would have involved a significant redesign for which the Army lacked funding, and would have delayed delivery when time was of the essence.

Into Action

The US Army would not employ the M2A4 in front-line service during the Second World War. Instead, it saw duty as a training vehicle in the United States. A total of thirty-six examples of the M2A4 went to the British Army.

The US Marine Corps also acquired thirty-six examples of the M2A4 in 1940 from the US Army. These saw combat with the Marine Corps during the fighting for the island of Guadalcanal, which lasted from August 1942 until February 1943.

On August 21, 1942 a platoon of five Marine Corps M2A4s attacked a defending Japanese infantry unit. American journalist and author Richard Tregaskis, then a war correspondent on Guadalcanal, recounted the attack in his classic book titled *Guadalcanal Diary*:

> It was like a comedy of toys, something unbelievable, to see them [tanks] knocking over palm trees, which fell slowly, flushing the running figures of men from underneath their treads, following and firing at the fugitives. It was unbelievable to see men falling and being killed so close, to see the explosions of Jap grenades and mortars, black fountains and showers of dirt near the tanks, and see the flashes of explosions under their very treads.

During the engagement, known as the Battle of the Tenaru, two of the Marine Corps' M2A4s were disabled, one due to a mine; their crews were rescued by the still operational tanks. Japanese losses to all American weapons came in at an estimated 800 dead and 15 taken prisoner, with only a few managing to escape the carnage.

M3 Light Tank Series

The next light tank acquired by the US Army proved to be the M3 series, a progressively improved version of the M2 light tank series. In total, 13,859 examples of the M3 series came off the factory floor between March 1941 and September 1943. There were three versions of the light tank: the original M3, the M3A1 and the M3A3. The M3 and M3A1 weighed about 14 tons and the M3A3 around 16 tons.

The M3 series, like the M2 series, rode on a Vertical Volute Suspension System (VVSS), which took its name from its volute spring. The spring was a helically-wound steel strip whose inner turns were arranged along the coil's central axis, giving the completed spring a conical shape.

The volute springs absorbed the compression load along their axis. Their advantages were that they were very compact when mounted in a road wheel bogie assembly consisting of two vertically-oriented volute springs. They were also very damage-resistant. When damaged, the broken components could still support a portion of the initial load.

The VVSS worked together with a track system designated the T16. It consisted of smooth rubber blocks (also referred to as pads) vulcanized around steel links connected with rubber-bushed steel track links. These

US Army Ordnance Department-developed design features first appeared on the T5 pilot Combat Car, initially tested in 1934.

Numbers

The most abundant of the M3 series tanks proved to be the original version, with 5,811 examples constructed. It was the most numerous model tank in the US Army's inventory when America officially entered into the Second World War, following the Japanese attack on Pearl Harbor (December 7, 1941).

Of the total number of the original M3 model tanks built, 1,285 received diesel engines rather than gasoline ones. The US Army only sent gasoline-engine-powered M3 series light tanks overseas, as it did not want to create a supply problem as all its other vehicles were gasoline-powered. Diesel-engine-powered M3 series light tanks not allocated for Lend-Lease (which began in March 1941) were reserved for training purposes only in the United States per a March 1942 directive. The second most numerous M3 series tank was the M3A1 with 4,621 built; 211 were powered by diesel engines. The M3A3s, of which 3,427 made it down the assembly line, were all powered by gasoline engines.

The thickest armor on the M3 series proved to be the CHA gun shield at 51mm (2in), except for the original M3's gun shield, only 38mm (1.5in) thick. The second-thickest armor on the tank, the CHA lower front hull, came in at 44mm (1.75in).

Marine Corps Light Tanks

The US Marine Corps also used the M3 series in the Philippines, with the first examples arriving in October 1942. However, they showed up with no spare parts and no reference material on how to order the spare parts required. The result was that some light tanks were stripped for spare parts to keep others running; this added to the problem of no skilled tank mechanics and no tools.

Those Marines' M3 series tanks came in both gasoline- and diesel-engine-powered configurations. The Marines preferred the diesel engine variants as diesel fuel proved more abundant in the Pacific Theater of Operations (PTO) due to its use by US Navy landing craft.

Marine Corps Marmon-Herrington Light Tanks

Both the M2A4 and M3 series were adopted by the Marine Corps instead of another light tank armed with a 37mm main gun. Its designer and manufacturer, Marmon-Herrington, could not meet the required delivery schedule.

The Marine Corps had acquired earlier machine-gun-armed versions of Marmon-Herrington light tanks in small numbers. These included the CTL-3 in 1936, the CTL-6 in 1941 and the CTM-3TBD in 1941. The first two were turretless, whereas the third had a turret; all rode on tracks and a suspension system similar to that on the M2A4 Light Tank.

All the Marmon-Herrington light tanks were considered under-armored and under-gunned. This is highlighted in a June 8, 1942 report by a Marine Corps captain to a superior officer. He wrote about his findings regarding the Marmon-Herrington light tanks:

> These tanks do not hold up under the strain of field conditions and are constantly breaking down during field training exercise ... The combat missions are very limited due to a minimum of armor, armament and speed. The armament would be of little effect against other tanks in combat.

Eventually the Marine Corps' senior leadership decided that the Marmon-Herrington light tanks were useless and had them all pulled from service in 1943. None of the tanks ever saw combat.

US Army Marmon-Herrington Light Tanks

Following the Japanese attack on Pearl Harbor, the American government seized all weapons intended for shipment overseas to foreign armies. Included were different versions of the Marmon-Herrington light tanks, both machine-gun-armed and those with 37mm main guns.

Some of the machine-gun-armed versions intended for the Nationalist Chinese Army entered US Army service as the T16 Light Tank. They never left the United States after their deployment along the country's western coastline including Alaska. Their usage was due to a fear of possible Japanese invasion following the attack on Pearl Harbor. When those fears dissipated, the Army removed all of them from service.

Two models of the Marmon-Herrington light tank armed with 37mm main guns, the CTMS-1TB1 and the MTLS-1G14 and intended for the Royal Netherlands East Indies Army, were tested by the Ordnance Department for possible use. However, due to their numerous design shortcomings, they were rejected.

Unofficial Nicknames

Design changes were continuous to both the original M3 and M3A1 while on the production lines. Unofficial nicknames therefore appeared to assist in identifying the sub-variants. These nicknames sometimes appear in American wartime military documents.

Diesel Engine Advantages

Diesel engines offered improved thermal efficiency, which in turn generated a greater range per gallon than their gasoline-powered counterparts. Diesel engines also delivered more torque at low engine speeds than gasoline engines, requiring fewer gear changes and thus less complex transmissions. A critical human safety factor in favor of diesel engines for combat vehicles is that it has a far higher flash point – the temperature at which the fuel will ignite – than gasoline.

For example, a sub-variant of the original M3 which lacked a tank commander's cupola became the 'low-profile' or 'streamlined' M3 in US Army service. The same tank in Marine Corps service received the nickname 'low top', while those M3 series tanks with the vehicle commander's cupola found themselves labeled 'high tops'.

Foreign Service

A total of 9,075 examples including all three versions of the M3 series were exported under Lend-Lease. The most numerous proved to be the M3A3, with 3,322 of the 3,427 built authorized for Lend-Lease.

Of the 5,473 M3 series tanks supplied to the United Kingdom, 2,045 were the M3A3. In decreasing order of assistance to the British Army were 1,784 examples of the original M3 and 1,594 of the M3A1. The British Army also received fifty diesel-engine-powered examples of the original M3 tank.

The Red Army received under Lend-Lease 1,676 examples of the M3 series, including 1,336 gasoline-engine-powered units and 340 gasoline-engine-powered M3A1s. The Red Army did not regard them highly because they considered them under-gunned and under-armored.

Of the other 1,926 examples of the M3 series allocated to Lend-Lease, the Chinese Nationalist Army received about 500. They were also supplied to the Australian Army and the Free French Army, among others.

In British Army Service

The British Army in North Africa received its first shipment of eighty-four examples of the M3 Stuart tanks in July 1941. From the War Diary of the 9th Queen's Royal Lancers are a few of the design disadvantages apparent to the British tankers upon their initial observation of the new tank:

1. No powered turret traverse system.
2. The awkward location of the manually-operated turret traverse mechanism.
3. No turret basket.

4. The tall driveshaft tunnel, which bisected the bottom of the fighting compartment, forces the two-man turret crew to step over it when the turret traverses.
5. The gunner often finds himself forced to turn over the aiming and firing of the gun to the vehicle commander/loader when the turret is turned at certain angles.
6. No periscopes in the turret, only direct vision ports, with armored shutters.
7. Neither the vehicle commander's overhead armored hatch nor the driver's or bow gunner's upper hull front armor shutters can be closed by the crewmen without assistance.

The British Army in North Africa quickly set about correcting as many of the Stuart's design issues as possible. By the time of their next major offensive (Operation CRUSADER, November 1941), it had in its inventory 453 examples. Most would be destroyed during the subsequent fighting due to poor tactical decisions made by all levels of British Army leadership when faced with a better-trained and better-led opponent.

British tankers did appreciate the Stuart's dependability, a hallmark of most American-designed and built wartime tanks. They unofficially nicknamed it 'the Honey'. The nickname appears in some British Army wartime documents, newspapers and tankers' post-war diaries.

British Army Tank Names

The British Army named its Lend-Lease-acquired M3 series tanks after the American Civil War cavalryman James Ewell Brown (J.E.B.) Stuart. Hence the M3 became 'General Stuart', typically shortened to just 'the Stuart' by British tankers.

On August 28, 1942 British Prime Minister Winston Churchill issued instructions on the naming of American tanks dictating that 'General' should no longer see use as it might cause confusion with active commanders.

A further British Army subdivision assigned each version of the Stuart series an added suffix. Gasoline-engine-powered examples of the original M3 came to be known as the Stuart I and the diesel-engine-powered models as the Stuart II. The M3A1 would become the Stuart III and the M3A3 the Stuart V.

An Office of the Chief of Ordnance document, dated November 24, 1944 and titled *Nicknames for Ordnance*, states that a policy had begun to adopt the British military naming system for tanks, not in official reports but for public information releases.

British tankers disliked the Stuart's short range and the poor ergonomics of its two-man turret arrangement. It also failed to measure up when confronted by better-armed and armored German medium tanks.

As more American-supplied medium tanks arrived for the British 8th Army in North Africa, the Stuart found itself pulled from front-line service and relegated to the less demanding role of reconnaissance.

The Stuart would remain in front-line service with the British Army in Asia, as well as with the Commonwealth Indian Army, until early 1945. Stuarts saw combat with the Australian Army in New Guinea between September 1942 and January 1943.

In American Service

To assist the US Army and the Philippine Army in building a credible defense force to deter Japanese aggression, two US Army National Guard tank battalions arrived on the main Philippine island of Luzon in 1941. Armed with 108 examples of the original M3, the two battalions formed the Provisional Tank Group under the command of Colonel James R.N. Weaver. Despite their best efforts there proved little they could do to stem the Japanese invasion of the Philippines, which began on December 8, 1942. They and all the other remaining American and Philippine military units surrendered on May 6, 1942.

Marine M3s in Action

As already mentioned, the Marine Corps employed eighteen of its M2A4s as well as M3s during the fighting for Guadalcanal.

As part of the invasion of Guadalcanal that began on August 7, 1942 the Marine Corps, with naval support, seized three nearby Japanese-occupied islands: Tulagi, Gavutu and Tanambogo.

Assisting Marine infantrymen assaulting Tanambogo on August 8, 1942 were two M3A1s from Company C of the 2nd Marine Tank Battalion. From the book *Follow Me* by author Richard W. Johnson is the following passage describing what the Marine tankers encountered:

> The tank commander drove his two light eggshell monsters inland, screaming Japs ran at the tanks with pipes and crowbars to jam the treads. Sweeney's guns were all going, and so were the guns of his companion tank, but there was a painful lack of room to maneuver. Rising from the turret to reconnoiter, Sweeney took a bullet through the head. The tank stalled and the crewmen fought their way out of it against Japs who were swinging knives and pitchforks.

The second Marine tank became entangled between two coconut palm tree trunks and was set on fire by the Japanese defenders carrying containers filled with gasoline. As the four-man crew attempted to escape their burning vehicle, the enemy attacked them with knives and bayonets. Two of the Marine tankers were killed, with the other two escaping with severe burns and numerous stab wounds. The next day the Marines counted forty-two Japanese dead around the burned-out M3A1.

Flame-Thrower M3A1

The usefulness of man-portable flame-throwers in dealing with Japanese Army defensive positions on Guadalcanal led to experimentation by both the Marine Corps and US Army with a tank-mounted version of the standard man-portable flame-thrower. The improvisation involved mounting the man-portable flame-thrower in place of the tank's bow machine gun. Trials with modified M3A1 tanks began in late 1942 and continued through 1943. Unfortunately the existing man-portable flame-thrower proved too fragile for sustained use from inside the tank.

In early 1944, a possible solution appeared when the US Army adopted a Canadian flame-thrower named 'the Ronson', designed specifically for use on vehicles. The Ronson had a range of 75 meters; nearly double that of a man-portable flame-thrower. As an experiment, an M3A1 had its 37mm main gun replaced by the Ronson in an April 1944 test.

The Marine Corps liked what they saw and had twenty-four M3A1 tanks rearmed with the Ronson in May 1944. In this configuration, the tank became known as 'the Satan'. The Marines had preferred mounting it in the M4 medium tank series, but none were then available.

The Satans first saw combat during the Battle for Saipan (June 15 to July 9, 1944), and then went on to see use during the Battle of Tinian (July 24 to August 1, 1944). From Special Technical Intelligence Bulletin No. 9 dated June 2, 1945 is this passage on the use of the Satans on Saipan:

> When a Japanese position held up the infantry, and could not be reduced by normal armored fire, it was the practice to hold the position under 75mm and machine-gun fire from two medium tanks while one of the M3 flame tanks burned it out. The flame weapons saw their major use in reducing cave positions and the interconnected machine-gun-and-sniper positions that infested Saipan cane fields. They were also used to burn away camouflage and heavy vegetation to clear fields of fire for other weapons.

Not Pleased

Though only Marine Corps M2A4s and M3 series were used on Guadalcanal, both Marine Corps and US Army assessment of their performance concluded that they were under-gunned and under-armored for the tasks assigned. This led to the conclusion that Sherman tanks would be a much better choice for both services in the Pacific Theater of Operations (PTO).

Marine Corps Brigadier General Robert L. Denig Jr. recalled his time on Guadalcanal: 'The light tanks were not heavy enough to push their way through the underbrush, and the small 37mm turret gun did not have enough charge in the ammunition to do much damage to emplaced machine-gun positions.'

The 37mm main gun on the M2A4 and M3 series fired fixed (one-piece) rounds of ammunition, including: AP (armor-piercing); APC (armor-piercing capped); HE (high-explosive); and Canister.

From the Catalog of Standard Ordnance Items, dated 1944, is a description of the canister round:

> The Canister Shot M2 is a terne-plate [thin steel sheet coated with an alloy of lead and tin] cylinder containing 122 3/8-in steel balls packed in resin. When fired, the casing breaks and the balls are ejected from the gun in the manner of a shotgun charge, to a maximum effective range of about 250 yards.

By the time of the Bougainville campaign, with the US military involvement running from November 1943 to November 1944, the Marine Corps had transitioned to the M3A1. For the invasion of the island of Betio, in the Tarawa Atoll, on November 20, 1943, the Marines employed two companies of M3A1s and, for the first time, M4 Sherman tanks.

The M3A1s proved a useful escorting for the M4A2 medium tanks around Betio, using their machine guns and canister rounds to keep Japanese defenders from trying to climb onto the tanks with explosives. However, after-action reports on the struggle for the island cemented the Marine Corps' opinion that the M3 series had little to contribute, and Sherman tanks replaced most of them in Marine Corps' tank battalions.

The M5 Light Tank

As aircraft received higher priority than tanks for the available output of lightweight, air-cooled radial engines in early 1941, the Ordnance Department began looking for an alternate source of engines. They were looking for one already in production to speed adoption.

The answer proved to be combining two General Motors liquid-cooled Cadillac automobile V8 engines, each coupled to an automatic transmission and installed in an M3 chassis. Seen in this passage from the official history of the US Army in the Second World War, in the volume titled *The Ordnance Department: Procurement and Supply*, the advantages of the Cadillac engine arrangement appeared:

> ... test reports on a Cadillac-powered model were favorable. Furthermore, the Cadillac engine was easier to start; it operated better at idling speeds; and the hydramatic [automatic] transmission made the tank driver's job much easier. In October 1941, a Cadillac-powered tank proved its durability by running under its own power all the way from Detroit [Michigan] to Aberdeen [Maryland], a distance of over 500 miles.

Setting up for production of the M5A1 at the Cadillac plant proved no easy task, as appears in the same volume: 'Makeshifts were the order of the day, for new equipment specially designed for tank production was virtually unobtainable. Because jigs and fixtures, so essential to mass production, take a long time to make, Cadillac did without them at the start, building its first tanks almost by hand.'

Although the Cadillac engine with liquid cooling proved to be 2,500lb heavier than the radial air-cooled engine of the existing M3, the advantages outweighed any disadvantages. Combined with a new RHA welded hull design upon which sat a modified M3A1 turret, the light tank design became the 16.5-ton M5. Production began in April 1942 and concluded in December 1942 with 2,074 examples completed.

The M5A1

The M5 would be followed off the assembly lines by a progressively improved version designated the M5A1, production of which began in November 1942 and ended in June 1944 with 6,810 examples built. The most noticeable M5A1 design change proved to be the adoption of a turret somewhat similar to that of the M3A3. The vehicle weighed approximately 17 tons. The lower front, made of CHA, had a thickness of up to 64mm (2.5in).

The US Army would employ the M5 series in the European Theater of Operations (ETO), the Mediterranean Theater of Operations (MTO) and the PTO until the end of the war, along with an ever-declining number of M3 series tanks.

An example of the M5A1 in action in the PTO appears in an Armored School research report titled *Armor in Operation Forager* (June 1944 to November 1944):

> The infantry and tank action continued to attempt to break through the enemy resistance on NAFUTAN. Phalon's platoon of light tanks

moved ahead of the infantry in order to flush the Japanese as if they were coveys of quail. Canister ammunition proved extremely valuable for this type of action when attempting to knock out positions placed in the brush or among the coral boulders ... The ammunition expended during the campaign shows that the light tanks fired much more than the medium tanks. HE and canister were employed more than any other. Very little smoke was used.

Unlike the US Army, the Marine Corps skipped the M5 and jumped directly to the M5A1 beginning in the summer of 1943. All were, however, pulled from service in favor of the Sherman tank's greater firepower, heavier armor, etc. in late 1944.

The British Army never received the M5 but did take into service 1,431 examples of the M5A1, which it designated the Stuart VI. Another five went to the Red Army, and 226 examples of the M5A1 were supplied to other friendly armies under Lend-Lease.

Flame-Thrower M5A1

During the 1944–45 fighting in the Philippines the US Army came up with an experimental tank-mounted flame-thrower based on the M5A1. The results appear in this extract from an Armored School Research Report titled *Armor on Luzon*:

The flame-thrower, E7-7, mounted in the M5A1 light tank proved effective in offensive operations against enemy dug-in positions. In addition to lowering the morale and completely demoralizing enemy troops, it had the distinct effect of raising the morale of our own troops when used as a supporting weapon. Due to the limitations of the light tank as to maneuverability, power and gradability, recommendations were later made for the installation of flame-throwers on a medium tank chassis.

Combat in North Africa

On November 8, 1942, under the code-name Operation TORCH, the US Army invaded French North Africa. Included among the American invasion forces were two armored divisions: the 1st and 2nd. Due to a lack of landing craft able to handle the M3 and M4 medium tanks, the first tanks ashore were the division's M3 and M3A1 light tanks. The M5 also arrived in North Africa in November 1942.

The only opponent for the US Army's light tanks was Vichy French forces, which included an armored element consisting of First World War-era light tanks. When encountered, the obsolete French tanks found themselves outmatched by the American light tanks and quickly fell to their betters. The Vichy French government leadership in North Africa agreed that the French military formations would submit and commence co-operating with the Allied forces on November 10, 1942.

The M5A1 Driver's Compartment

Michael Panchyshyn, a volunteer at the Virginia Museum of Military Vehicles, has this to say about starting up the M5A1 Light Tank:

The M5A1 is like a skateboard on tracks. Or a go-kart. It just gets and goes because two Cadillac automobile engines power it with a Hydra-Matic [automatic] transmission.

Getting into the driver's station is very easy on the M5A1 compared to its predecessor, the M3A1. The roof-mounted hatch is still very small for the modern-day driver, though. We have to remember the GIs driving these Stuarts in the 1940s were much smaller than the average person now, having grown up during the Great Depression.

Once inside, the driver's compartment is very roomy, wide in the shoulders and leg area compared to many tanks. The first thing to notice is that the steering levers are pivoted at the top, not on the bottom like most tanks. A small instrument panel is in front of the driver. On it are the typical gauges: RPM, oil temperature, etc.

There are two ignition switches and two starter buttons – one for each of the Cadillac engines. Behind the driver's left shoulder is the Master electrical switch. That is very important to have in the ON position, otherwise the batteries are cut off from the electrical circuit and the tank won't start.

After making sure the steering levers are pulled back to engage the brake, the Master is turned on. The ignition switch for the left engine is turned on, and the starter button is engaged. The engine is so quiet, the only real indication it is working is the increased breeze thru the driver's hatch, as the engine gulps air.

The second ignition switch is turned to the on position and the starter engaged, up comes the second Cadillac engine, purring smoothly. The engine RPMs are synchronized, brakes released, and the forward high gear is selected on the Hydra-Matic transmission.

The driver's seat is adjustable, but only to two positions. The upper position is with the hatch open and head exposed. The lower position would be used for combat, with the hatch closed. To see out, the driver would peer through a rotating hooded periscope.

The next encounter that American light tanks had with enemy armor occurred on November 26, 1942 and did not go nearly as well. On that occasion, they confronted better-armed and armored German medium tanks. A young lieutenant described what happened when one of his light tanks opened fire on a nearby German Mark IV medium tank:

> ... the German [tank] commander soon spotted his heckler ... and leisurely commenced closing the 140-yard gap between himself and the [American] light tank, but keeping his thicker, sloping frontal plates turned squarely to the hail of 37mm fire. The crew of the M3 redoubled the serving of their piece ... Tracer-tailed armor-piercing bolts streaked out of the American's muzzle and bounced like a mashie [golf club] shot ... from the plates of the Mark IV. In a frenzy of desperation and fading faith in the highly-touted weapon, the M3 pumped more than 18 rounds at the Jerry tank while it came in. Through the scope sight, the tracer could be seen to hit and glance straight up.

The engagement ended when the German tank fired an armor-piercing (AP) round through the front hull of the American tank, killing the driver. As the remaining members of the crew bailed out of their tank, the loader fell to enemy machine-gun fire. However, the tide of battle quickly turned when the German medium tanks turned their thinner-armored sides and rears to an unseen number of nearby M3 light tanks that riddled them in short order. The final score turned out to be six M3s destroyed and seven German medium tanks.

A Rethink of Light Tank Roles

By the end of the fighting in North Africa in May 1943, it was clear that US Army light tanks were not up to operating as the offensive spearhead of armored divisions. At the same time, the Army's senior leadership decided to make some significant changes to most of its armored divisions' TO&Es.

Among those changes, the number of light tanks dropped from 158 to just 77. They were assigned the supporting role, and the medium tanks became the offensive spearhead of the 1943 armored divisions.

Some questioned the requirement for any light tanks at all, something that occurred throughout the remainder of the war, but found themselves overruled. In some tank battalions, the light tanks were not even employed. In other units, the crews of the light tanks acted as replacements for losses in the Sherman tank companies.

From the After-Action Report of the 759th Light Tank Battalion of fighting in the ETO between July 1944 and March 1945 is a passage on the M5 series light tanks:

... [it] is apparent that a light tank battalion, armed with only 37mm guns, unless very skillfully employed with Infantry, will suffer severe casualties in men and material. The Light Tank still has to depend on speed, maneuver and selection of suitable targets if it is to be of very much use. In spite of the fact that the training of this Battalion was not pointed toward reconnaissance lines, we have been able to accomplish our missions with a Cavalry Reconnaissance Group with a much greater degree of success than in any other assignment to date.

Brigadier General Albin F. Irzyk of the 4th Armored Division would be asked in a May 2014 interview how he employed his light tank:

If we're moving rapidly and the enemy is scattered, we put the light tanks out. We usually had a troop of cavalry attached to us. So it would be the cavalry and the light tanks out front with the medium tanks behind them. During the Battle of Chaumont, I had them on both flanks.

2nd Armored Division Impressions

In a March 1945 2nd Armored Division report titled *United States vs German Equipment* there is a quote by Lieutenant Colonel Wilson M. Hawkins regarding the M5 series light tanks:

The light tank is being used for working with the infantry. We subject it to direct fire just as little as we can, for it is realized that the armor will not turn the German fire or the 37mm gun damage the German tanks or SP [self-propelled] guns.

In the same 2nd Armored Division report, tank commander Sergeant Benjamin S. Palczewski commented:

Our M5A1 light tanks do not have tracks wide enough to keep them from bogging down in soft ground. I had my tank bogged down in a field east of Julich, Germany, on February 28, 1945. I noticed the track prints of a German Panther tank (Pz.Kw. V) running parallel to the bogged position. A Panther weighs 45 tons, our M5A1 only 15 tons.

Some Positive Comments

Some felt that the light tanks could be useful in combat, as seen in this passage from an Armored School monograph titled *The First Armored*

Division Breakthrough at Anzio, dated April 19, 1948. In it, an officer of the 135th Infantry Regiment is quoted as saying:

My men are really sold on those tanks. They are really enthusiastic about the way those tanks worked right along with them, especially the light tanks. They are still talking about the way those light tanks darted around like a bunch of bees and every time a doughboy [American soldier] called, a light tank would come from nowhere and help him out. 'We'll fight with 1st Armored tanks any day.'

In an Army report, *Lessons from the Italian Campaign*, dated March 15, 1945, the commander of the 3rd Battalion, 1st Armored Regiment, describes how his light tanks operated with infantry during the fighting at Anzio:

Light tanks stayed right with the infantry where they were able to knock out those positions which the medium tanks had by-passed: positions such as well-concealed machine-gun nests and enemy personnel with automatic weapons, which can do very serious damage to the infantry. The light tanks, moving with the foot troops, caused the enemy in these positions to give up readily. The infantry used green smoke grenades to call attention of the light tanks to the fact that the individual had a target which he wanted to point out to the tank. Any light tank was to proceed to the location of the smoke and be directed by the individual who set off the smoke as to just what the target was.

In the After-Action Report of the 756th Tank Battalion describing its actions between May and June 1944 during the Italian campaign is this passage describing a minor engagement:

> As the light tanks moved out of Carpineto, heavy anti-tank fire was encountered, and the second tank in the column was destroyed by a penetration. The first tank was immobilized by a hit which knocked out the ignition system on the tank, but which fired at suspicious-looking points ahead. (This fire destroyed a German Mark IV tank, though this was not discovered until the tank burst into flames. Three 37mm penetrations of the Mark IV were later found.)

Although some British reconnaissance units would employ M3A1s and M3A3s through to the end of the fighting in the ETO by the time of the invasion of France in June 1944, the US Army had switched to the M5 series light tanks.

Despite having been relegated to secondary roles, light tanks could still prove useful on occasion, as seen in this passage from an After-Action Report of the 24th Cavalry Reconnaissance Squadron from June 6, 1944 to June 27, 1944:

> The 37mm anti-tank gun, mounted in all armored cars [M8] and tanks, proved an extremely useful and effective weapon in this campaign against enemy personnel and equipment. Its accuracy with HE ammunition and the destructive power at close quarters and in

hedgerow areas with canister ammunition far surpassed the expectations of the using troops; they gained respect for the gun as the campaign progressed. Its power of penetration with AP ammunition was extremely limited employed against enemy fortifications, however.

The T7 Light Tank

Well aware that the M2A4 light tank configuration had limited capacity for significant improvement, the Armored Force identified a requirement and issued a list of characteristics for a new light tank. It was not to weigh more than 14 tons and have a maximum frontal armor thickness of 38mm (1.5in), with the main armament a 37mm gun.

The proposed new light tank received the designation T7. Many different versions also appeared, each with different design features indicated by suffixes. As development progressed, however, the estimated weight of the T7 rose to as much as 16 tons.

The first T7 pilot appeared in January 1942, powered by an air-cooled radial engine. Both its turret and hull were CHA. When presented with a wooden mock-up of a proposed low-silhouette version of the T7 series, the Armored Force decided that was what they wanted.

As of January 1942, a decision came about to arm the T7 series with a 57mm main gun. When the 57mm main-gun-armed version of the T7 showed up for testing in May 1942, its weight had risen to 26 tons.

A New Designation

Lieutenant General Jacob L. Devers, commander of the Armored Force, was unhappy with the 57mm main gun on the T7. He asked for a 75mm main gun in June 1942. At this point, the Armored Force had begun to consider the T7 as a possible replacement for the M4 medium tank series.

In August 1942, before any testing of a 75mm main-gun-armed T7 took place, the vehicle would find itself standardized as the M7 Medium Tank and orders were placed for 3,000 examples. Devers referred to it as 'the tank of the future'.

The Ordnance Department had thirteen production examples of the T7 Medium Tank built, with the first six reserved for testing purposes. They showed up for trials in December 1942.

When combat-loaded, the M7 Medium Tanks now weighed almost 29 tons, an unpleasant surprise. An effort began to lower the vehicle's weight; however, at that point, it was clear that the M7's performance during testing showed it to be inferior in almost every way compared to the existing M4 series medium tanks. Production of the M7 ended in April 1943.

Another Overweight Light Tank

The M7 Medium Tank dead end was not the only example of an Ordnance Department light tank that could not keep the weight off. In August 1942, the Ordnance Department got together with the Armored Force to consider another light tank design, which eventually received the designation T21. It would be a lighter version of the experimental T20 Medium Tank.

The Armored Force wanted the T21 to weigh no more than 20 tons, armed with a 75mm gun, later changed to a 76mm main gun, and to have enough armor to protect it from .50 caliber machine-gun fire. Early thinking envisioned it as using the suspension system of the T7 Light Tank. It also had to have a top speed of 35mph and a cruising range of 150 miles.

By the time the final layout drawings of the T21 were complete, the Ordnance Department had estimated that a completed pilot of the tank would weigh up to 25.5 tons. Well aware that proposed tanks always gain weight during their development cycle, the Armored Force pulled the plug on the program without building a pilot vehicle. Ordnance canceled the program in the summer of 1943.

The M22 Light Tank

In February 1941, a meeting took place between the Ordnance Department, the Armored Force and the Air Corps. The topic of conversation was a requirement for a small, lightweight tank for use by both American and British Army airborne forces. The proposed vehicle received the designation Light Tank T9 and was to feature either a 37mm or 57mm main gun. What eventually evolved from the T9 turned out to be the 37mm main-gun-armed M22 Light Tank weighing in at around 8 tons.

Authorization for the construction of 1,900 examples of the M22 soon came about. However, as events transpired, it became apparent that the tank was under-armed, under-gunned and worse, unreliable. The US Army lost interest and production of the M22 found itself capped at 830 vehicles, built between April 1943 and February 1944.

As the British Army had a sufficiently large glider to transport a single example of the M22, a total of 260 of the airborne tanks went to them under Lend-Lease. The British Army assigned the M22 the official nickname 'Locust' and used a few of them in combat with some success. At the same time, those remaining in the US Army inventory went into storage until eventually going to the scrap dealers in the early post-war years.

M24 Light Tank

Despite the T7 Light Tank failure, the Armored Force still wanted a better-armed and better-armored light tank to replace the M5 series. The

Ordnance Department worked with Cadillac to incorporate the power-train from the M5 series into the design, along with a new suspension system and broader tracks. The Ordnance Department had experimented with wider tracks for the M5 series without success.

As initially proposed, the new light tank would come with a 57mm main gun. However, a new lightweight, low-velocity 75mm main gun, adapted from an aircraft ground-attack weapon, became part of the design. The gun bore the designation of the 75mm Gun M6. The vehicle had, at this point, received the designation T24 Light Tank.

Tests of the initial pilot T24 proved so positive that the Ordnance Department authorized the production of 1,000 examples in October 1943 instead of M5A1s. The order was subsequently increased to 5,000 examples of what became the M24 Light Tank in July 1944.

An example of what convinced the Ordnance Department and the Armored Board to order so many M24s so quickly appears in an extract from a US Army report titled *The Armored Force Command and Center* and subtitled 'Army Ground Forces Study No. 27, 1946':

> On a cross-country course considered to be the toughest of its kind, constructed over a route consisting of steep grades, side slopes, rocky areas, timbered zones for sharp turning tests, sandy ground and stumps and fallen trees, the Armored Board tested the M24, together with eleven other armored vehicles. Of the 12 vehicles, only three actually completed the course. In the tank class, the M4 medium tank made the grade in three hours and twenty minutes, and the M24 finished with no difficulty in two hours and sixteen minutes ... From these and similar tests the Board concluded that the M24 light tank was superior to any known type of light tank in durability, reliability and general field-worthiness.

More Details

The M24 had a crew of four men, later increased to five. Both the tank's turret and hull consisted of RHA. Armor protection proved extremely limited to keep the vehicle's weight down to 20 tons. The turret gun shield topped out at 38mm (1.5in) and the front glacis 25mm (1in).

Production of the M24 began in April 1944 and ended in August 1945, with a final vehicle count of 4,731 examples, of which, 291 were consigned to Lend-Lease, with the British receiving 289 and 2 going to the Red Army.

The British Army assigned the M24 the official nickname of 'the Chaffee' after US Army Major General Adna Chaffee, the first commander of the Armored Force who died of cancer on August 22, 1941. The M24s provided to the British Army did not arrive in the ETO in time to see combat, but were present for the follow-on victory parades.

Into Combat

The first examples of the M24 arrived in the ETO in December 1944 and were met by US Army tankers with excitement. An example of that appears in a document titled *Immediate Report No. 83*, subtitled 'Combat Observations' and dated December 19, 1944. The following comment was made by Major H.J. Samuel of the 4th Cavalry Group: 'The superiority of the M24 over the M5 in firepower, maneuverability, increased flotation and lower silhouette has greatly increased the striking power of cavalry units. We were able to employ them as assault guns and use our assault guns as supporting artillery.'

Samuel would also mention in the report a few issues that he felt needed to be addressed: 'It is essential that the .50 caliber machine gun be mounted on the front of the turret rather than the rear to permit easy firing by the tank commander.' He went on: 'Apparently, a larger recoil guard is needed on the 75mm gun. Two of our men have had arms broken by the recoil.'

Good and Bad

Despite the light weight of the M24 and its wider tracks and torsion bar suspension system, it would find itself out-classed in mobility by the Panther tank. A quote by Colonel Paul A. Disney of the 2nd Armored Division reads: 'During a recognition demonstration, a captured German Mark V Panther demonstrated that it could turn faster than the M24 light tank, move as fast as the M24 on ordinary terrain, and had a lower silhouette.'

The M24 had a sting, as seen in the same report, in a quote by Sergeant J.C. Johnson, tank commander:

A German Mark V Panther started across my front at a range of 800 yards. I gave my gunner a fire command to open fire with armor-piercing. The first round hit the German Mark V, stopping it and setting it afire. I had my gunner fire an HE [high-explosive] shell next which hit the tank and the fire increased. The next round, which was white phosphorous, made the tank explode.'

(**Above**) The beginning of the US Army's search for a suitable pre-war light tank proved to be the T2E2 Light Tank pictured. It rode on a modified version of a British-designed suspension system employing all-steel tracks and leaf springs. The US Army's displeasure with the suspension system led to a re-working of the vehicle with a strengthened volute spring suspension system, leading to the designation T2E2. (*Patton Museum*)

(**Opposite, above**) In this 1934 photograph, we see the experimental T2E2 Light Tank, which eventually became the M2A2. Visible is the vertical volute spring suspension (VVSS) system and the T16 rubber-block track system. These two design features became the standard for US Army pre-war and wartime light and medium tanks. (*TACOM*)

(**Opposite, below**) On display at the Mississippi Armed Forces Museum is a four-man M2A2 Light Tank. One of the two turrets had as its armament a .50 caliber machine gun, then considered a more than adequate anti-tank weapon. In the other turret and the bow gun in the tank's sloped glacis were .30 caliber machine guns. The roughly 9.5-ton tank had a top speed on level roads of 45mph. (*Pierre-Olivier Buan*)

ROCK ISLAND ARSENAL

731-40661   Nov. 16, 1935
Light Tank, T2E2

(**Above**) Seen here is an M2A3 Light Tank. Essentially an improved M2A2, the tank had slightly thicker frontal armor, with its bogie wheel suspension units spaced out from 87in to 97in to reduce ground pressure and improve mobility. Also the rear hull configuration was changed to improve access to the gasoline-engine-powered radial engine. (*Pierre-Olivier Buan*)

(**Opposite, above**) The M1 Combat Car pictured here belonged to the US Army's Cavalry Branch. It had a diesel-engine-powered counterpart designated the M2 Combat Car. Both used the same basic chassis as the US Army's Infantry Branch M2A2 and M2A3 Light Tanks. The major external difference was the cavalry's preference for a single two-man turret. (*Patton Museum*)

(**Opposite, below**) The Spanish Civil War (1936–39) saw combat introduction of the German-designed and built 3.7cm (37mm) Pak 36 towed anti-tank gun pictured here. It dominated tank warfare during the conflict and set the benchmark for frontal armor protection levels of the US Army's pre-war and early-war light and medium tank designs. (*Pierre-Olivier Buan*)

RA PD 4747

(**Opposite, above**) In response to reports from the Spanish Civil War, the US Army ordered the M2A4 Light Tank, an up-armored and up-gunned version of the M2A3 Light Tank. Due to its length, the 37mm Gun M5's recoil mechanism protruded from the cast homogenous armor (CHA) M20 Combination Gun Mount. Protecting it required the addition of an armored sleeve, as appears here. (*Patton Museum*)

(**Opposite, below**) User feedback and testing revealed a number of design problems with the M2A4 Light Tank. Fixing those issues resulted in the introduction of the M3 Light Tank, the first production example of which is pictured here. The rear idler was enlarged and lowered to ground level, as seen in this image, to reduce the vehicle's ground pressure. Note the turret's riveted construction. (*TACOM*)

(**Above**) During its production run, the M3 Light Tank sported three different turret designs: the first, all riveted face-hardened armor (FHA); the second (pictured here), consisted of FHA armor plates welded together, except for the bolted front turret plate. It, too, was eventually changed to a welded FHA plate. (*Patton Museum*)

(**Above**) On this M3 Light Tank the only forward vision provided to the driver and bow gunner with their front upper hull hatches closed was provided by two direct vision slots visible in this picture. The turret cupola had six vision slots. The tank's turret also had three armored pistol ports, one of which is behind the closed flap that appears in this image. (*Patton Museum*)

(**Opposite, above**) The vehicle shown here has the final M3 turret design of welded rolled homogenous armor (RHA). To serve two purposes, the three armored pistol ports on late-production M3 Light Tank turrets incorporated a periscope vision device (referred to as a protectoscope) and the ability for the turret crew to engage close-in enemy infantry with their small arms. (*Patton Museum*)

(**Opposite, below**) Early-production M3 Light Tanks had a single-piece hatch cover on the turret cupola, which could only open forward. Due to its weight and size, the vehicle commander could not close this without outside assistance. To correct that design flaw, later-production M3 Light Tanks had the new two-piece split hatch cover visible on this vehicle's cupola. (*Patton Museum*)

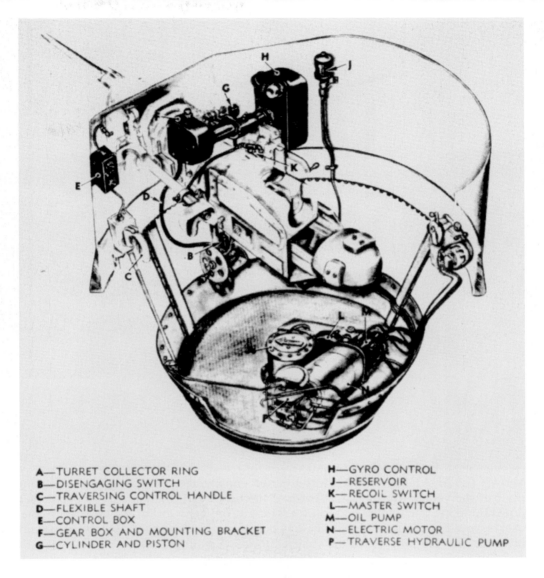

A—TURRET COLLECTOR RING
B—DISENGAGING SWITCH
C—TRAVERSING CONTROL HANDLE
D—FLEXIBLE SHAFT
E—CONTROL BOX
F—GEAR BOX AND MOUNTING BRACKET
G—CYLINDER AND PISTON

H—GYRO CONTROL
J—RESERVOIR
K—RECOIL SWITCH
L—MASTER SWITCH
M—OIL PUMP
N—ELECTRIC MOTOR
P—TRAVERSE HYDRAULIC PUMP

(**Opposite, above**) Running through the center of this M3 Light Tank's fighting compartment is the very high drivetrain enclosure, through which a propeller shaft connected the rear hull compartment's radial engine to the front hull-mounted transmission. As the vehicle had no turret basket, the vehicle commander/loader and gunner had to step over or on it as they manually traversed the turret. (*Pierre-Olivier Buan*)

(**Opposite, below**) The next vehicle developed in the M3 Light Tank series proved to be the M3A1 Light Tank pictured here. A key identifying feature of the tank is the absence of a vehicle commander's cupola. It was replaced by two small overhead hatches. The commander had a rotating periscope forward of his hatch. (*Public domain*)

(**Above**) At the British Army request, the M3A1 Light Tank had a power-operated turret traverse mechanism, including a turret basket as pictured here. Both the vehicle commander and gunner sat on seats that rotated with the turret. Another feature added was a gyrostabilizer that worked in elevation only. (*Patton Museum*)

(**Above**) The M3A1 Light Tank's turret basket endangered the bow gunner. He could only exit the vehicle via the turret hatches, the turret had to be in certain positions to allow him to get out, and he had to wait for the turret crew to exit the tank first. Otherwise, he could not escape. The driver, by comparison, had a two-piece forward-folding hatch that allowed him to exit the vehicle quickly if required. (*Richard and Barb Eshleman*)

(**Opposite, above**) On this M3A1 Light Tank, we can see the outboard armored hoods for the driver's and bow gunner's protectoscopes. Inboard are the direct-vision slots for the driver and bow gunner with their outer moveable armor covers in the closed position. Late-production M3 Light Tanks had the same arrangement. On the tank's turret were the same three protectoscopes incorporated into the turret's pistol ports that had first appeared on late-production M3 Light Tanks. (*Pierre-Olivier Buan*)

(**Opposite, below**) A diagram of authorized storage for an M3A1 Light Tank. Included were 103 rounds of 37mm ammunition, including armor-piercing (AP), high-explosive (HE) and anti-personnel canister rounds. There was also space for 8,270 rounds of .30 caliber ammunition and 12 hand grenades. (*Patton Museum*)

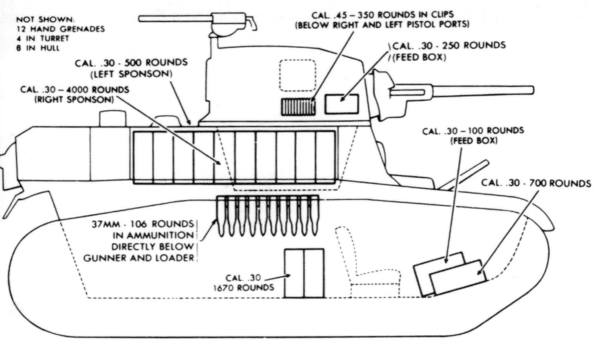

NOT SHOWN:
12 HAND GRENADES
4 IN TURRET
8 IN HULL

CAL. .45 — 350 ROUNDS IN CLIPS
(BELOW RIGHT AND LEFT PISTOL PORTS)

CAL. .30 - 250 ROUNDS
(FEED BOX)

CAL. .30 - 500 ROUNDS
(LEFT SPONSON)

CAL. .30 — 4000 ROUNDS
(RIGHT SPONSON)

CAL. .30 – 100 ROUNDS
(FEED BOX)

CAL. .30 - 700 ROUNDS

37MM - 106 ROUNDS
IN AMMUNITION
DIRECTLY BELOW
GUNNER AND LOADER

CAL. .30
1670 ROUNDS

(**Above**) At a certain point, production of new M3A1 Light Tank turrets, identified here by the absence of a turret cupola, outstripped that of the M3A1 Light Tank chassis. Mating the M3A1 turret minus its turret basket to the existing M3 Light Tank chassis resulted in the vehicle pictured here and referred to by modelers and researchers as the Interim M3. A spotting feature is the vehicle's retention of .30 caliber sponson machine guns. (*PICRYL*)

(**Opposite, above**) In April 1942, the Armored Force requested that the proposed M3A3 Light Tank should have a hull somewhat similar to that of the M5 Light Tank that had just entered production. The M3A3 welded hull consisted of RHA plates. It was also fitted with a new longer turret with room in the rear bustle for a radio, following British Army practice. All M3A3s went for Lend-Lease. (*Pierre-Olivier Buan*)

(**Opposite, below**) Following the Japanese attack on the US Navy base at Pearl Harbor, the US government took control of all foreign contracts involving military equipment. Among the already-built weapons intended for foreign clients but not yet shipped over-seas were several models of light tanks built by the American firm Marmon-Herrington. The CTLS-4TAC, designated by the US Army as the T16 Light Tank pictured here, saw only limited service. (*Patton Museum*)

(**Opposite, above**) The Marine Corps had experimented with a variety of light tanks designed and built by the Marmon-Herrington Company since 1935. The vehicles tested were all small machine-gun-armed vehicles such as the CTL-6 pictured here. Eventually the Marines gave up on the very unreliable Marmon-Herrington light tanks and adopted the US Army's more robust M3 series. (*Patton Museum*)

(**Opposite, below**) The constant shortfall of gasoline-engine-powered radial engines for the M3 Light Tank series led to the M5 Light Tank series, an example of which is pictured here. Power came from two Cadillac car engines, combined with a newly-designed hydramatic (automatic) transmission. Accommodating the new twin-engine arrangement required a much larger engine compartment, as seen here. (*Chris Hughes*)

(**Above**) The M5 Light Tank series' most noticeable external design feature was the 48-degree sloped glacis seen in this photograph. This feature was borrowed from the M3A3 Light Tank design. The M5 Light Tank retained the M3A1 Light Tank's turret design and the 37mm Gun M6 that had first appeared on the M3 Light Tank in mid-production. (*Pierre Olivier Buan*)

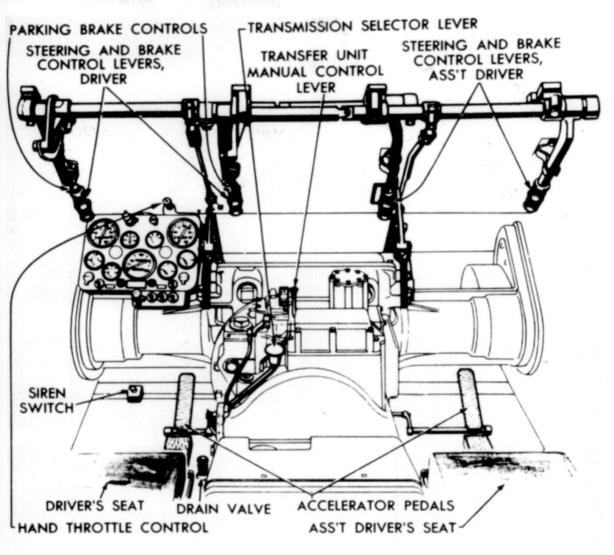

PARKING BRAKE CONTROLS

STEERING AND BRAKE
CONTROL LEVERS,
DRIVER

TRANSMISSION SELECTOR LEVER

TRANSFER UNIT
MANUAL CONTROL
LEVER

STEERING AND BRAKE
CONTROL LEVERS,
ASS'T DRIVER

SIREN
SWITCH

DRIVER'S SEAT

HAND THROTTLE CONTROL

DRAIN VALVE

ACCELERATOR PEDALS

ASS'T DRIVER'S SEAT

(**Opposite, above**) The M5 Light Tank's sloped glacis plate provided enough room to install overhead hatches for the driver and bow gunner, as seen in this image. Each overhead hatch incorporated a rotating periscope. The driver and bow gunner were provided with direct vision via two 51mm (2in) holes in the glacis that were sealed with the steel plugs shown here and secured with attached chains when buttoned up. (*Pierre-Olivier Buan*)

(**Opposite, below**) At a certain point in the M5 Light Tank's production run, a design modification fitted the vehicle with a version of the M3A3 Light Tank's longer turret. This design received the designation M5A1, with an example pictured here. The M3A1 turret's pistol ports with their protectoscopes were quickly eliminated during the M5A1's production. (*Author's collection*)

(**Above**) Unlike previous light tank designs in which only the driver could operate the vehicle, the M5 Light Tank series provided duplicate driving controls for the bow gunner as an assistant driver, as seen in this diagram. The location of its steering laterals also differed from earlier light tanks, which had them floor-mounted. (*Patton Museum*)

(**Opposite, above**) A late-production feature on the M5A1 Light Tank is the enclosure fitted to the turret's right-hand side, as visible in this photograph. It stored the vehicle's .30 caliber machine gun when not in use. Another late-production feature was a large storage container fitted onto the rear of the engine compartment. (*Hans Halberstadt*)

(**Opposite, below**) In this image, we see the restored turret of an M5A1 Light Tank. The gunner sat on the left of the 37mm Gun M3, and the vehicle commander/loader on the right. For aiming the main gun, the gunner had the Telescope M40, clearly visible in the center of the photograph, and the M4 Periscope seen to the upper left. (*Hans Halberstadt*)

(**Above**) In January 1944, the US Army tested the concept of a turretless M5A1 Light Tank in the reconnaissance role, armed with a .50 caliber machine gun, as pictured here. The project went nowhere, however, as a next-generation light tank armed with a 75mm gun made more sense. (*Patton Museum*)

(**Opposite, above**) With some user feedback on the M2A4 Light Tank, the Armored Force compiled a list of desirable design characteristics they wanted to see in the new light tank design, designated the T7. Several pilots with different design features appeared, including the T7E2 pictured here. However, the tank's ever-increasing weight led to it being redesignated the Medium Tank M7. In that role it was unsatisfactory, leading to its cancelation in 1944. (*Patton Museum*)

(**Opposite, below**) The Chief of Staff of the US Army, General George M. Marshall, had a strong interest in creating airborne formations. Developmental work began on a specialized light tank to provide them with some measure of armor-protected firepower. The result was the M22 pictured here. (*Pierre-Olivier Buan*)

(**Above**) It became clear to the British and American armies during fighting in North Africa (1942–43) that the M3 and M5 series light tanks were badly under-gunned. Work began on a new up-gunned light tank armed with a 75mm main gun. It received the designation of the T24. Production began in April 1944 and the vehicle became the M24 as pictured here. (*Richard and Barb Eshleman*)

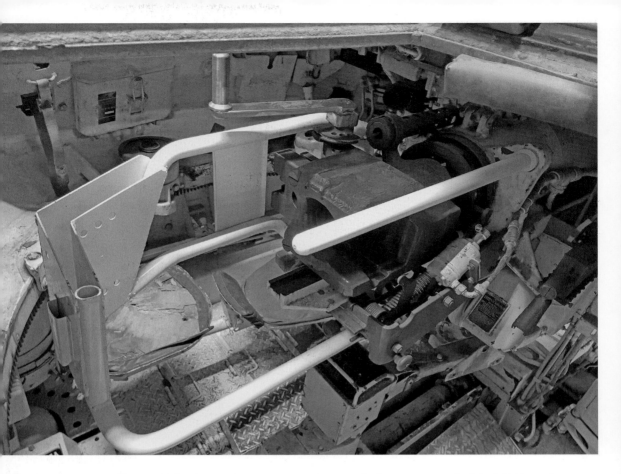

(**Opposite, above**) With the engine compartment roof plate removed, this M24's twin eight-cylinder Cadillac engines are visible. Rather than the VVSS of previous light tanks, the M24 rode on a torsion bar suspension system with 16in-wide tracks. On a level road, a top speed of 35mph could be attained. It had a range of approximately 100 miles. (*Pierre-Olivier Buan*)

(**Opposite, below**) The M24 Light Tank's Ordnance Department-designed torsion bar suspension system consisted of ten individually-sprung dual road wheels: five duals on either side of the vehicle. With shock absorbers fitted to the first two and last two road wheels, it could cross an 8ft trench and climb a vertical wall 36in high. (*Ian Wilcox*)

(**Above**) Looking down the vehicle commander's hatch of an M24 Light Tank, with the 75mm main recoil guard dividing the turret. The gunner sat on the left-hand side of the main gun and the loader on the right. Authorized storage consisted of 48 rounds of 75mm ammunition and 440 rounds for the turret's roof-mounted .50 caliber machine gun. (*Pierre-Olivier Buan*)

Chapter Two

M3 Medium Tank Series

The beginning of the M4 series of medium tanks can be traced back to May 21, 1936 when the US Army Ordnance Committee recommended the development of what would become the T5 Medium Tank series. It was a scaled-up version of the 13-ton M2A1 Light Tank. As with previous light tanks, the medium tank would have a gasoline-powered, air-cooled, radial engine.

The 1937 prototype of the T5 Medium Tank consisted of a riveted soft-steel hull riding on an enlarged version of the already proven Vertical Volute Suspension System (VVSS) that had first appeared on the US Army Cavalry T5 Combat Car in 1934. The VVSS also used the T16 track system made up of smooth rubber blocks (referred to as pads) vulcanized around steel links held together by rubber-bushed track pins.

The prototype T5 Medium Tank had a wooden upper hull and turret armed with dummy weapons. The soft-steel replacement for the wooden mock-up of the T5 appeared in 1937 with the designation T5 Medium Tank, Phase I. The maximum weight of the vehicle was 15 tons. Anything more substantial would have exceeded the load-carrying capacity of most American bridges, as well as the US Army's portable bridges.

Original armament for the T5 Medium Tank, Phase 1, consisted of a dummy 37mm gun (a production example was not yet ready) and eight .30 caliber machine guns. The latter comprised four in the front upper hull, two in the rear upper hull and two attached to the turret for anti-aircraft protection. A bit later, the dummy 37mm gun was replaced by two 37mm guns in a side-by-side mount.

The Next Step

With some minor modifications, including the replacement of the twin 37mm guns with a single 37mm gun, the T5 Medium Tank, Phase 1, was standardized on June 2, 1938 with the designation M2 Medium Tank.

The M2 Medium Tank retained the eight .30 caliber machine guns of the T5 Medium Tank Phase 1. The large numbers of machine guns on the vehicle were insisted upon by the US Army Infantry Branch, which until the forming of the US Army Armored Force in July 1940 heavily influenced the attributes of tank designs.

Unlike the soft steel construction of the T5 Medium Tank, Phase 1, the M2 Medium Tanks came off the assembly line with FHA and a more powerful gasoline-powered, air-cooled, radial engine. The vehicle's stood at around 19 tons. Production of the first eighteen examples began in the summer of 1939 at the government-owned and operated Rock Island Arsenal, with fifty-four more examples authorized for production in 1940.

Continued Development of the T5 Medium Tank

Despite the US Army standardizing on the M2 Medium Tank in June 1938, the Ordnance Department continued to experiment with the T5 Medium Tank series, including a version labeled the T5 Medium Tank, Phase III. There was no Phase II example of the vehicle.

With the Phase III version of the T5 Medium Tank, the Ordnance Department began testing the concept of improving the vehicle's automotive performance, as well as increasing armor protection levels without exceeding a maximum weight limit of 20 tons.

The inputs for the up-armored T5 Medium Tank Phase III came from the Spanish Civil War (1936–39). The conflict saw the widespread employment of towed 37mm and 47mm high-velocity anti-tank guns, which would have easily penetrated the frontal armor of the T5 Medium Tank, Phase 1, which ranged from 1in at its thickest portion down to 0.25in.

Another experiment with the T5 Medium Tank, Phase III, involved fitting it with a 75mm light artillery howitzer in the vehicle's right front upper hull. It could fire either semi-fixed (two-piece) high-explosive (HE) ammunition or a semi-fixed, high-explosive anti-tank (HEAT) round. With the 75mm howitzer fitted, the vehicle became the T5E2 Medium Tank.

French Tank Influence

The French Army had proven the feasibility of mounting a 75mm cannon in the front upper hull of a tank with the introduction into service in 1935 of their Char B1 Heavy Tank. The vehicle also had a high-velocity turret-mounted 47mm gun.

Unlike the 75mm howitzer that went into the T5E2 Medium Tank, optimized for firing HE rounds, the 75mm gun of the French tank was a dual-purpose weapon, firing both a fixed (one-piece) armor-piercing (AP) and a fixed high-explosive (HE) round.

Fearing future German military aggression, the French government had provided plans for the Char B1 Heavy Tank to American industry in 1940 and inquired if it could build an improved version of their tank. The US Army denied the French request. It only wanted tanks constructed in the country acceptable to its own requirements.

In place of a turret armed with a high-velocity 37mm gun, the T5E2 Medium Tank had a much smaller one-man turret fitted with an optical range-finder and armed with a single .30 caliber machine gun. Testing of the 75mm howitzer-armed T5 Medium Tank took place between April 1939 and February 1940. It proved it to be a practical solution for fitting into a medium tank if so required.

M2 Medium Tank Series

Testing of the Medium Tank M2 had led to the quick decision that it needed to have thicker armor and be fitted with an up-rated gasoline-powered, air-cooled, radial engine. The maximum armor thickness of the front upper hull, consisting of welded RHA, increased to 1.25in. These upgrades brought the vehicle's weight up to approximately 21 tons.

Also the original turret of the M2 Medium Tank with the inward-sloping armor surface proved too cramped and resulted in a new roomier turret design with vertical sides. All the improvements applied to the M2 Medium Tank resulted in the designation M2A1. The lower hull, as with the T5, consisted of RHA plates riveted together.

With the advent of the M2A1 Medium Tank, the US Army decided that instead of having fifty-two examples built of the M2 Medium Tank in 1940, it wanted them to be of the M2A1 configuration. However, German military successes in Poland in September 1939 and France and the Low Countries in the summer of 1940 led the US Army to reconsider the numbers and types of tanks required.

Up until the time the German military overran France and the Low Countries, the small number of US Army tanks ordered came out of the government's Rock Island Arsenal. In foreseeing a possible future situation calling for far more tanks than could be built at Rock Island, the US Army had envisioned arranging contracts with American commercial firms to build tanks if needed. The answer proved to be affirmative, and industry received the blueprints on June 17, 1940 for the three pilot examples of the M2A1 Medium Tank built by the Rock Island Arsenal.

The US Army wanted 1,000 examples of the M2A1 Medium Tank constructed. In the end, only ninety-four examples of the vehicle came off the assembly line between December 1940 and August 1941.

An Armament Change

Not long after the US Army placed contracts for 1,000 examples of the M2A1 Medium Tank, the US Army became aware of the German Army Pz.Kpfw. IV Medium Tank. British Army reports labeled these as the Mark IV. All other German tanks in British Army reports, and in later

American military reports, found themselves described by the term 'Mark' followed by a number suffix.

The early Mark IV had a short-barrel, turret-mounted, 75mm gun/ howitzer, which immediately made the US Army's M2A1 Medium Tank obsolete. The German tank gun was not an anti-tank weapon. Instead, it was a support weapon to engage enemy positions with high-explosive (HE) rounds and to support the Mark III Medium Tank which was originally armed with a high-velocity 37mm gun and later a 50mm gun.

In response to the knowledge gained of the 75mm cannon-armed German medium tank, the Ordnance Committee met with Major General Adna R. Chaffee (the first head of the Armored Force). He decided that the M2A1 Medium Tank needed a front-upper hull-mounted 75mm cannon, as demonstrated with the experimental T5E2 Medium Tank.

The M3 Medium Tank

A proposed version of the M2A1 Medium Tank, armed with an upper hull-mounted 75mm gun and a turret-mounted 37mm gun was standard-ized on July 11, 1940 as the M3 Medium Tank. Standardization occurred before the design drawings for the vehicle were approved.

The decision on having a front-upper hull-mounted 75mm gun in the M3 Medium Tank and not a turret-mounted example was not based on US Army preference. Instead, it reflected the fact that industry could not then make a turret large and robust enough to house a 75mm gun and deal with the weapon's recoil forces. However, industry indicated it would not take much longer to develop that capability.

The US Army infantry branch initially wanted to retain the eight .30 caliber machine guns of the M2A1 Medium Tank for the M3 Medium Tank. However, that did not prove practical and the number eventually dropped to just three .30 caliber machine guns. Of the three .30 caliber machine guns on the M3 Medium Tank, one resided in the lower front upper hull, another in the turret and a third in the vehicle commander's cupola. Besides the redesign of the front upper hull for the fitting of a 75mm gun, the M3 was to feature thicker armor, bringing the vehicle's weight up to approximately 30 tons.

M3 Armament

The 75mm gun chosen for fitting into the M3 Medium Tank was a failed Army Coastal Artillery anti-aircraft gun design designated the T6. The tank gun version's original designation was the 75mm Gun T7. It later became the 75mm Gun M2. It went onto the M3 series only as a temporary measure, awaiting a longer-barreled version.

Homogenous Armor

Rather than the FHA of the M2 Medium Tank series, the initial production versions of the M3 Medium Tank series were built from two different types of homogenous armor: rolled and cast.

Rolled Homogenous Armor (RHA) proved easier and less costly to produce than FHA, and if adequately sloped it offered the same resistance to penetration as FHA. Unlike FHA, RHA is essentially uniformly hard throughout its depth and has a very high degree of ductility.

According to an extract from the US Army Green Book series, listed as The Technical Services and entitled *The Ordnance Department: Procurement and Supply*: 'An additional advantage was that homogeneous armor had less tendency toward "back spalling", i.e. splintering of the back under the impact of a projectile. As a result, homogenous armor was authorized for all areas where a sloped surface could be presented to the enemy.'

A disadvantage of RHA is its inability to form easily other than in flat plates. Subsequently, manufacturing complex shapes with RHA plates increases costs. Therefore, cast homogenous armor (CHA) comes into play as it could mold into almost any shape desired, such as tank hulls as well as turrets. It can also be formed in varying thicknesses in a single pour, with weight distribution allocated to sections that are most vulnerable to enemy projectiles.

In 1939, an American firm designed and constructed a one-piece experimental CHA tank upper hull, supposedly the first of its kind. In June 1941, a 6-ton CHA hull was approved for the M3 Medium Tank. Due to its resemblance to a bathroom fixture, it became known as the 'inverted bathtub for elephants'.

A disadvantage of CHA is that it must be thicker, hence heavier because it lacks the toughness added by the work-hardening process of RHA. This negative is partly offset by the rounded surfaces that mark CHA, which increase the chances of incoming projectiles glancing off.

The longer-barreled version of the 75mm gun received the designation M3 when it appeared. It fired an HE round as well as two different types of AP rounds: the M61 Armor-Piercing Capped-Tracer (APC-T) round at 2,030 ft per second, and the M72 Shot-Tracer (AP-T) round, with the same muzzle velocity. The term 'shot' refers to a solid steel projectile with no explosive filler.

The term 'capped' referred to a forged blunt steel alloy cap that fits over the normal steel nose of a projectile. The cap reduced the amount of stress

Types of 75mm HE Fuzes

The HE round fired from the 75mm Gun M3 had two fuze settings, as appears in a 1943 War Department manual dated April 22, 1943 entitled *Tank Gunnery*:

(1) Super-quick action: The super-quick action is so sensitive that the shell detonates immediately on impact. Therefore, when striking armor plate, a gun shield or a building, the shell will burst before it can penetrate. The super-quick burst is effective against personnel in the open.

(2) Delay action: The .05-second delay action results in the shell penetrating before bursting when it strikes light armor, gun shields or buildings. If the shell strikes the ground, it ricochets, travels 20 to 25 yards beyond the point of impact, and then bursts about 10 feet in the air. Because of the down spray from the burst in the air, a ricochet burst has devastating effect on personnel without overhead cover.

upon impact with an enemy tank's armor. It did so by transferring the energy over a larger area, for a longer period preventing the steel projectile behind it from shattering. This allowed it to penetrate the armor of an enemy tank.

The M-61 APC-T round had a small hollow space for an HE filler, but due to production delays none were available until near the end of the Second World War. Upon the addition of the HE filler and a base detonating fuze, the round became the Armor-Piercing Capped, High-Explosive-Tracer (APC-HE-T). Covering the front of the ballistic cap was a thin metal aerodynamic windscreen that improved its in-flight characteristics.

What the US Army referred to as an APC round, the British Army labeled Armored-Piercing, with Armor-Piercing Cap and Ballistic Cap (APCBC). Due to widespread use of APC/APCBC rounds, the Germans switched from FHA to RHA on their tanks between 1942 and 1943.

The Role of the M3

It's important to note that at the time the M3 Medium Tank was initially proposed, the 75mm gun was considered a supporting artillery piece and not an anti-tank weapon. In 1940/41, light tanks and not medium tanks were considered the critical striking force of armored divisions.

The turret-mounted 37mm gun (originally the M5 and later the M6) in the M3 series was considered the vehicle's anti-tank gun. It fired an APC round at a muzzle velocity of 2,900 ft per second. Unfortunately, German tank designs continued to evolve throughout the Second World War with ever-thicker armor becoming the norm, rendering the 37mm gun obsolete as an anti-tank weapon by 1941.

Getting it Built

It would take until February 1940 before the first design drawings of the M3 Medium Tank emerged. Even after that, numerous design changes occurred. The pre-production pilot of the new medium tank, completed by the Rock Island Arsenal, rolled off the arsenal floor in March 1941. Vehicle weight had risen at this point to around 30 tons.

Four companies eventually undertook production of the M3 medium tank series. Three of them were railroad manufacturers, including the

---

American Industry Goes to War

In Charles K. Hyde's book titled *The Arsenal of Democracy: The American Automobile Industry in World War II* and Arthur Herman's *Freedom's Forge* is an often told but very poignant story about the state of the US military in the 1940s. In August 1940, William Knudsen was in a meeting with both American and British officials regarding supplying Britain with much-needed weapons of war, especially tanks. 'There was concern that American Car & Foundry was barely making thirteen a month.' Members of the meeting started asking about other locomotive companies and whether they could assist.

Before America entered into the Second World War, Knudsen was a prominent automobile industry executive. Upon the country's involvement, President Franklin Roosevelt appointed Knudsen as director of production for the US war effort and made him a lieutenant general.

Knudsen asked 'What about a car company?' The thought had never occurred to the members present. They asked Knudsen if they would help. Knudsen, the former president of General Motors, picked up the phone and asked for Detroit. Knudsen knew that the war could not be won without the mobilization of Detroit and its workforce, facilities and expertise on assembly-line production.

Knudsen was connected with K.T. Keller, the president of Chrysler Motors. 'We have a problem, K.T. We have to make more tanks than any corporation has ever made in the past. Can you do it?' Keller's response was typical of the can-do spirit of the time. 'Sure. When can we meet?' 'Tomorrow,' said Knudsen and flew to Detroit the next day. They spent a day discussing a new plant and laying out production lines, machines and other equipment. Yet despite Keller's enthusiasm, neither he nor his engineers had ever seen a tank!

American Locomotive Company, the Pressed Steel Car Company and the Pullman Standard Car Company. The fourth commercial firm was an automobile builder, the Chrysler Corporation, which formed the Chrysler Tank Division in 1940. All their tanks were constructed at the government-built and owned Detroit Tank Arsenal, which they managed.

It took until April 1941 before the first pre-production pilots from the various commercial firms tasked with building the vehicle were ready for testing. Upon the Ordnance Department approving the different pre-production pilots, series production began the same month. By December 1941, American factories had completed 2,591 medium tanks.

Production of the first-generation M4 Medium Tank series ramped up during the summer of 1942. Production of the M3 Medium Tank series did the opposite, with the last examples coming off the assembly lines in December 1942. By the time production of the M3 series ended, American factories had built 6,258 examples of the vehicle, divided between six different models.

It's important to note that the US Army never considered the M3 series as anything other than a class of interim vehicles before the fielding of a suitable medium tank with a turret-mounted 75mm main gun, which of course became the M4 series.

British Army Needs

With the fall of France and the loss of most of its tanks, the British Army, like the French Army before it, inquired of American industry if it would be willing to build British-designed tanks in its factories. The US Army informed the British Army that it would only allow them to order American-designed tanks for their own use, such as the M3 Medium Tank.

However, the US Army did allow for some requested modifications to the British Army's order for M3 Medium Tanks. These included a redesigned fighting compartment and a new larger British-designed turret. The reason was that US Army policy at the time was to have the vehicle's radio in the hull, whereas British Army policy called for the radio to be in the rear of the turret, which the American-designed turret could not accommodate.

To differentiate between the two different versions of the original model of the M3 Medium Tank, the British Army referred to the US Army-configured model as 'General Lee I' and their version as 'General Grant I'; hereafter, they were respectively labeled 'the Lee' and 'the Grant'. The latter would come off the production line between August 1941 and July 1942.

Not Everybody was Happy

Chaffee did not think very highly of the M3 series. He recommended that only a few hundred should come out of the factories. He wanted to wait until such time when industry could design and manufacture a turret large enough to house a 75mm gun. That turret could then fit onto a modified chassis of the M3.

Chaffee was, however, overruled as his superiors believed that stopgap M3 series remained better than nothing, if only for training purposes. In addition, the British required as many medium tanks as possible for the North African campaign that had begun in June 1940. Whatever the shortcomings of the M3 Medium Tank, it proved superior to the existing British Army tank designs, both in armor and firepower.

M3 Versions

The most numerous of the six models of the M3 Medium Tank series proved to be the initial model, the M3, with 4,924 examples constructed between June 1941 and August 1942. Among that number were both those in the US Army Lee configuration and the modified configuration of the British Army Grant.

The production examples of the M3 Medium Tank, both the Lee and the Grant, featured riveted upper and lower hulls, side upper hull doors and gasoline-powered, radial, air-cooled engines. Refinements were made to the design as production continued.

The M3's thickest armor topped out at 51mm (2in) on the front of the sloped upper hull glacis and sloped CHA turret. Both the upper and lower hulls consisted of RHA plates riveted together. The disadvantage of riveted armor plate appears in a March 21, 1950 US Army report entitled *The Vulnerability of Armored Vehicles to Ballistic Attack*:

> Tests of riveted joints, however, proved that, with the advent of larger-caliber projectiles with greatly increased velocities, rivets would not be able to withstand efficiently the severe shocks that would impart to armor. It was found that, when an impact was located near a line of rivets, the portion on the inside of the vehicle was likely to fly off with considerable velocity, causing possible injury to the crew.

The development of five other variants of the M3 Medium Tank series, other than the original M3 Medium Tank, came about to address production bottlenecks. These included a shortage of gasoline-powered, air-cooled, radial engines and the need to simplify production which in turn would reduce cost and speed up production.

M3A1 through M3A3

The 300 examples of the M3A1 built between January 1941 and July 1942 featured a CHA upper hull and a riveted RHA lower hull. The turrets on all six models of the M3 series were constructed of CHA and armed with a 37mm gun, including the British-designed turret for the Grant.

More of the M3A1 might have come out of the factories, but not enough foundry capacity proved available at the time. Power came from a gasoline-powered, air-cooled, radial engine for all but the last twenty-eight built. These, in a failed experiment, had a diesel engine fitted. Those powered by the diesel engine bore the designation of the M3A1 (Diesel). The British Army never took delivery of the M3A1 or the M3A1 (Diesel).

The M3A2 had an all-welded RHA upper and lower hull. Just twelve examples built between January and March 1942. Power came from a gasoline-powered, air-cooled, radial engine. None went to the British Army.

A total of 322 examples of the M3A3 came off the assembly lines between March and December 1942. The M3A3 had the same all-welded upper hull and welded lower hull of the M3A2. Like the M3A2, the M3A3 received power from a twin diesel-engine arrangement. The British Army referred to it as 'the Grant II'.

M3A4 and M3A5

The M3A4 was identical to the original version of the M3. Instead of a gasoline-powered, air-cooled, radial engine, it had five Chrysler liquid-cooled, gasoline-powered truck engines, coupled together and referred to as the A-57 Multibank. Some 109 examples came off the assembly line between June and August 1942. None went to the British Army.

As with the M3A3, the M3A5 received power from a twin diesel-engine arrangement. However, rather than the all-welded RHA upper hull of the M3A3, it had an all-riveted upper hull with a lower RHA riveted hull. A total of 591 examples of the M3A5 came out of the factory doors between January and December 1942. As with the diesel-powered M3A3, the British Army designated the M3A5 'the Grant II'.

Who Got What?

Of the 6,258 examples of the M3 series constructed, around 1,600 came off the factory floor in the Grant configuration. Besides the M3 Medium Tank, the Grant turret also appeared on the M3A3 and M3A5. Due to combat losses, the British Army would also take into service 1,347 examples of the Lee tank configuration.

The Australian Army would ultimately receive 757 examples of the M3 series, both in the Lee and Grant configurations. All were shipped directly from American factories to Australia under British War Office providence. The majority saw use as training vehicles. The British Army would eventually pass on 900 examples of the Grant to the Indian Army. The British Army would employ the Lee tank in fighting the Japanese in Burma between 1942 and 1943.

American factories would ship the Red Army 1,386 examples of the M3 series in the Lee tank configuration. Of that number, 417 never made it to the Soviet Union due to enemy action; i.e. submarine or aircraft attacks. The Red Army did not think very highly of their Lee tanks and quickly relegated them to secondary theaters of combat.

First Impressions

A small number of Grant tanks reached the British Army in North Africa in November 1941. By May 1942, the British Army had 167 examples of the vehicle on hand. British tankers were excited by the American-built medium tank, even though it was too tall due to the awkward arrangement of the vehicle's two guns and the limited traverse of its 75mm gun.

Early problems encountered and dealt with on the Grant tank revolved around its 75mm ammunition. These included the age of the HE ammunition, making them dangerous to fire, incorrect fuzes for HE rounds, and lack of an AP round. The British solved this by adapting captured German 75mm AP projectiles to fit onto US Army-supplied 75mm cartridge cases.

Another problem discovered by the British tankers with the Grant tank was that their engines began overheating after only twenty-five hours of running time, a concern quickly corrected. With that issue solved, the Grant tank eventually proved to have a much higher level of automotive reliability than existing British Army tanks.

An important advantage of the Grant over existing British tanks then in service was that its 75mm gun fired a decent-sized HE round. This allowed British tankers, for the first time, to successfully engage enemy towed anti-tank guns, a standard element of German Army combined arms operations. Existing British Army tank guns fired only AP shot rounds. The tank's hybrid 75mm AP rounds could penetrate the frontal armor on German tanks at a range of up to 400 yards.

Into Combat

The first encounter between the British Army's Grant tank and their German Army counterparts in North Africa took place at the end of May 1942. The latter suffered heavy losses, which proved a shock to senior

German officers in North Africa. The British tankers were impressed by the amount of punishment the Grant tank could take in battle. One vehicle supposedly survived thirty-one hits by enemy 37mm and 50mm guns.

The battlefield advantages of the American Grant/Lee tanks began to wane in August 1942 with the German introduction of a new version of their Mark IV Medium Tank, the Pz.Kpfw. IV Ausf. F2. It sported a very potent, long-barreled 75mm gun that could easily penetrate the frontal armor on the Grant tank at a range of 1,110 yards with its AP rounds.

While the up-armed German medium tanks began appearing in North Africa, enough M4 series medium tanks had arrived in theater to out-number the Grant tanks available for service. As the M4 series lacked the major design drawback of the Grant tank, its front-upper hull-mounted 75mm gun, it quickly became the British Army's tank of preference.

American Combat Experience with the Lee

Most Lee tanks employed by the US Army served as training vehicles in the United States. As new armored divisions were to be shipped overseas, the Lees found themselves replaced by the Sherman. The only exception was the 1st Armored Division that left for Ireland in May 1942. Its medium tank battalions still had their Lee tank when the movement took place. The reason: their intended M4 series tanks were diverted at the last moment to the British Army fighting in North Africa.

When plans came about for Operation TORCH, the invasion of French North Africa in early November 1942, it included Lee tanks from the 1st Armored Division. They would be the first US Army medium tanks to encounter the German Army in North Africa beginning at the end of November into early December 1942. As with most encounters between the combat-inexperienced and combat-wise, the latter prevailed, inflicting heavy losses on the former.

Lieutenant Colonel Henry E. Gardiner of the 1st Armored Division describes what he remembered when his M3 tank received a hit: 'There was a blinding flash in the tank, a scream and I had been hurt. I jumped out of the tank and ran back a short distance and crouched. There had been seven of us in the tank and I saw four get out.'

The condition of the M3 tanks in the 1st Armored Division aggravated the problem. They had suffered from extensive wear during training exer-cises before Operation TORCH, and combat operations quickly eroded the pool of operational M3s as no replacements arrived. Lack of spare parts also made it challenging to keep the remaining Lee tanks functional.

The divisional commander of the 1st Armored Division wanted to restrict his Lee tanks to secondary duties only, such as training vehicles, acting as gunnery targets or clearing minefields. Brigadier General Paul M. Robinett who commanded an armored regiment of the 1st Armored Division, initially equipped with the M3 during the North African fighting, wrote in his 1958 autobiography *Armored Command*:

> Our M3 medium tanks were no match for the German Mark IV ... There were many bad features that damned our tanks. The German tanks had greater mobility on soft or sandy terrain. Our M3 medium tanks were higher than German tanks and presented a better target ... The lack of all-round traverse made the medium tank [M3] extremely vulnerable in a running fight and in a withdrawal. The armor-piercing ammunition of the German 75mm gun penetrated from 4.1 to 5.9 inches of steel plate at 1,000 yards, normal impact; while the best American ammunition would penetrate 3.5 inches only ... American tactical doctrine and training were, therefore, out of line with reality.

The only other fighting that the Lee saw with the US Army during the Second World War occurred between November 20 and 23, 1943, on the other side of the world. A US Army tank battalion, still equipped with the Lee, supported a US Army infantry division in the capture of the Japanese-defended island of Butaritari, a part of the Makin Atoll.

The Ordnance Committee recommended an experimental medium tank designated the T5 in May 1936. The initial development resulted in two pilots labeled the T5 Phase I and the T5 Phase III; the former is pictured here. Pilot testing began in 1938. (*Pierre-Olivier Buan*)

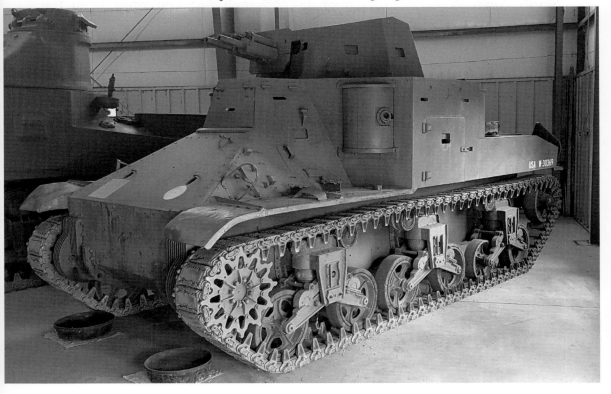

(**Opposite, above**) To test the concept of mounting a more powerful weapon in the T5 Medium Tank Phase III, the T5 Phase I was extensively modified. A small machine-gun-armed turret fitted with an optical range-finder replaced the original turret, and a 75mm Howitzer M1A1 was installed in the superstructure on the right side as pictured here. (*Patton Museum*)

(**Opposite, below**) Following satisfactory test results, the T5 Medium Tank Phase I was standardized (approved for production) as the Medium Tank M2, with some changes. Instead of the original twin turret-mounted 37mm guns, the M2 had only a single 37mm gun. Pictured here is the driver's position on the centerline of an M2. (*Patton Museum*)

(**Above**) The sides of the Medium Tank M2's two-man turret sloped inward, with the turret roof sloped both front and back. The vehicle's turret and hull were face-hardened armor (FHA) supported by structural steel angles and held together by nickel-steel rivets. The glacis had a thickness of 46mm (1.8in), with the hull floor coming in at 12mm (0.5in). (*Patton Museum*)

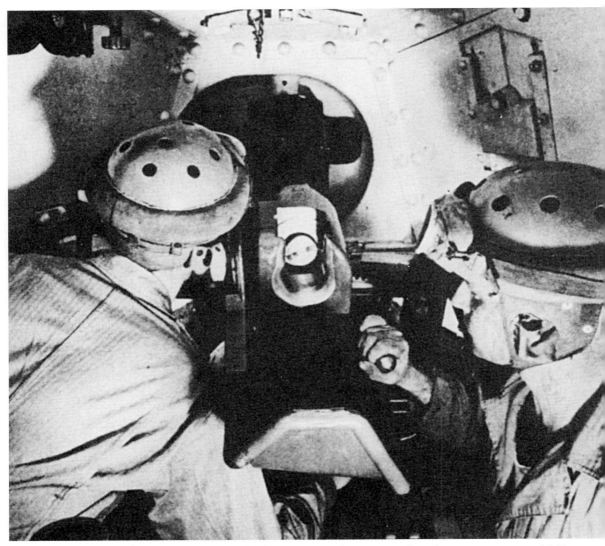

(**Above**) The crew on a Medium Tank M2 is seen here operating the turret-mounted M3 37mm main gun, a version of the infantry's towed 37mm Gun M3, which entered service in early 1940. Its breechblock was manually-operated. The crewmen are wearing the infantry-style tanker's helmet issued in 1937. (*Patton Museum*)

(**Opposite, above**) Eventually supplementing the Medium Tank M2 would be the M2A1 pictured here. Besides slightly thicker armor, the biggest difference between the Medium Tank M2 and the Medium Tank M2A1 was the large, roomier turret of the latter, constructed of vertical FHA plates. (*TACOM*)

(**Opposite, below**) The successful German invasion of France in the summer of 1940 shocked the US Army. That led to standardization of the Medium Tank M3, which was armed with a front hull-mounted 75mm gun in July 1940. The pilot example appears in this picture. (*TACOM*)

The design of the Medium Tank M3 proved heavily influenced by the French Army Char B1 bis Heavy Tank seen here. The US Army, like the French Army, saw the M3's 75mm gun as a supporting weapon capable of firing high-explosive (HE) rounds, and the turret-mounted gun as the vehicle's main anti-tank weapon. (*Pierre-Olivier Buan*)

The US Army Medium Tank had a 360-degree traversable vehicle commander's cupola armed with a .30 caliber machine gun, as seen here. The French Army Char B1 Heavy Tank's commander had only a fixed ventilation cupola on the turret roof, and entered and exited the vehicle via a large fold-down armored hatch on the back of the turret. (*PICRYL*)

A worker poses with an individual suspension assembly unit for an M3 Medium Tank, which had three suspension units on either side of the hull. Each consisted of two rubber-tired suspension wheels, two vertically-oriented volute (coil) springs protected by the large volute suspension bracket that is the body of the assembly. At the top of each suspension assembly unit sat a single return rotor. (PICRYL)

As an M3 Medium Tank passes over uneven terrain, the vertical movement of the two bogie wheels of each suspension assembly unit is transferred to the supporting arm or levers and absorbed by the two volute springs. The drive sprockets at the front of the tank pull the tracks forward from the rear, directing them down and in front of the advancing individual suspension assembly units. The track return rollers support and carry the upper run of each track. (Patton Museum)

(**Above**) Earlier production examples of the M3 series of medium tanks featured a large armored door on either side of the upper hull, provided to allow crewmen in the hull to enter and exit on either side. Incorporated into each door was the complex periscope-like device seen here from the interior, referred to as a protectoscope. (*Richard and Barb Eshleman*)

(**Opposite, above**) The US Army version of the two-man CHA of the M3 series medium tank had a thickness of approximately 51mm (2in), with the turret roof at 22mm (0.875in). The front of the turret gun had a slope of 47 degrees and the sides only 5 degrees. (*Pierre-Olivier Buan*)

Early-production examples of the M3 series of medium tanks came off the factory floor with the 75mm Gun M2 pictured here. It had a length from breech face to muzzle of 7ft 6in. The original plans, however, called for the longer-barreled 75mm Gun M3 that had a length from breech face to muzzle of 9ft 9in. Using the same ammunition as the M2, the M3 with its longer barrel had a higher muzzle velocity, increasing armor penetration. (*Pierre-Olivier Buan*)

Looking at the interior components of a 75mm Gun M2. The gun could be manually traversed 15 degrees left or right from center. Note the gunner's hand wheels for elevation/depression and traverse. The gun could be elevated 20 degrees and depressed 9 degrees. It also had a stabilizer system for elevation only. (*Pierre-Olivier Buan*)

The 37mm gun-armed turret of the M3 series medium tank pictured here had a stabilizer system for elevation only, plus a power traverse system. The combination of the two features in 1941 testing demonstrated that it greatly increased the effectiveness of the 37mm gun at speeds up to 10mph. (*Dreamtime*)

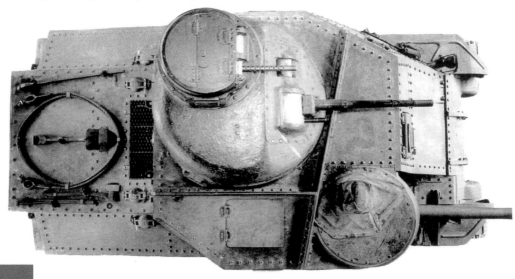

An air-cooled, gasoline-powered, radial engine is pictured here going into a Medium Tank M3. The official designation for the engine was Wright (Continental) R975 EC2. On a level road, the vehicle could reach a top speed of 21mph, although maximum speed for short periods on level roads was 24mph. *(Patton Museum)*

(**Above**) Looking in at the driver's position on an M3 Medium Tank from the right-side armored door. Note that his seat straddles the vehicle's front hull-mounted transmission. The synchromesh transmission provided the driver with five speeds forward and one in reverse. The tank's cruising range was approximately 120 miles. (*Pierre-Olivier Buan*)

(**Opposite, above**) When members of the British mission arrived to purchase American tanks under Lend-Lease, they accepted the M3 but requested various changes. While the US Army did not accept all requested changes, to minimize production delay, it did allow a different turret design. The British felt that the tank was too tall, providing a larger target area, and wanted the commander's radio mounted in a turret bustle as in other British tanks. The British Army officially labeled tanks in the configuration pictured here as 'the General Grant I'. (*Pierre-Olivier Buan*)

(**Opposite, below**) With the gun mount removed, we can see the No. 19 radio set in the rear turret bustle of a Grant tank. Unlike American tank radio sets that were frequency-modulated (FM), British radios were amplitude-moderated (AM). Those M3 series medium tanks taken into British Army service, which retained the US Army-configured 37mm gun-armed turrets, were officially named 'the General Lee I'. This was normally shortened to just 'the Lee'. (*Patton Museum*)

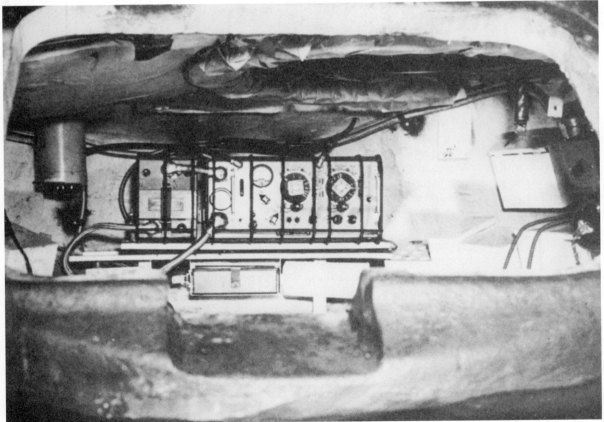

(**Above**) A late-production M3 Medium Tank fitted with the longer-barrel 75mm Gun M3. Note that the tank lacks the upper hull side armored doors. That feature was discontinued on the production lines as it created a weak spot in the tank's armor protection, and the change reduced production effort, time and cost. (*Richard and Barb Eshleman*)

(**Opposite, above**) American industry and the US Army constantly explored different ideas for improving and simplifying M3 Medium Tank production. One of these involved replacing the riveted RHA upper hull of the M3 Medium Tank with a CHA upper hull, as seen in this picture. In this configuration, the vehicle received the designation of the M3A1 Medium Tank. (*TACOM*)

(**Opposite, below**) Enemy projectile impacts could break rivets, causing the rivet head to ricochet in the interior, damaging equipment or killing or wounding the tankers. Bullet splash – the liquification of a bullet striking the armor – could enter the tank via riveted seams, with the same effects. To eliminate this, the US Army ordered an all-welded upper hull, assigning the resulting vehicle the designation Medium Tank M3A2. (*Patton Museum*)

(**Opposite, above**) Pictured here is an example of a welded upper hull M3 series medium tank powered by a twin diesel truck-engine arrangement that was labeled by the manufacturer as the Model 6046. With this engine configuration, the vehicle received the designation M3A3 Medium Tank. A shortage of gasoline-powered radial engines used for the riveted-hull M3 Medium Tanks led to their being fitted with the Model 6046 and receiving the designation M3A5. (*Pierre-Olivier Buan*)

(**Opposite, below**) On the shop floor of the Virginia Museum of Military Vehicles (VMMV) is this restored General Motors Model 6046 twin-diesel-engine powerplant. The two six-cylinder engines weigh 5,110lb and are liquid-cooled. Top speed for the M3A3 Medium Tank on level roads was 25mph, although for short distances on level roads a maximum speed of 30mph was possible. (*Paul and Loren Hannah*)

(**Above**) In another attempt to power the M3 series of medium tanks, there appeared the M4A4 as pictured here. It received power from five Chrysler gasoline-powered car engines combined into a single power pack referred to as the A57 Multibank. Due to the increased size of the engine arrangement, the upper and lower hull of the vehicle had to be lengthened and enlarged in specific locations. (*TACOM*)

Chapter Three

Early War M4 Tanks

When the Ordnance Committee standardized the M3 Medium Tank series in July 1940, it also directed that work should begin on an upgraded medium tank. The intention was that the new design should incorporate as many M3 design features as possible to expedite production of the new tank, such as the M3's suspension system and gasoline-powered, air-cooled, radial engine.

In August 1940, the Armored Force provided a detailed listing of the design characteristics it wanted to see in the upgraded medium tank, which included a CHA turret-mounted 75mm gun and a reduction in vehicle height.

Work on the upgraded medium tank had to wait until the Ordnance Department finished its efforts on the M3 series, an endeavor that took until February 1941. That same month, a meeting took place to confirm the design features of the upgraded medium tank, which included the retention of the M3 series' lower hull design as well as its suspension system and automotive components.

The Lead-Up

In May 1941 the Ordnance Committee recommended the construction of a full-scale wooden mock-up along with a pre-production pilot vehicle featuring a CHA upper hull and riveted RHA lower hull, designated the T6 Medium Tank. It was to include a CHA turret armed with a 75mm gun.

By the following month, the Ordnance Committee decided it also wanted a second pre-production T6 pilot, this time with a welded RHA upper hull but no turret. That request reflected the fact that there remained insufficient foundry capability to cast CHA upper hulls for all the anticipated new medium tanks.

The pre-production T6 pilot was ready for inspection on September 2, 1941. The most noticeable design feature that the new vehicle shared with the M3 series was the armored hatches (doors) on either side of the upper hull. These were intended for escape on either side. The Armored Force, however, wanted these removed as they were a weak spot in the tank's armor protection.

The M4 Medium Tank Appears

Upon the completion of inspection of the approximately 30-ton T6 on September 5, 1941, the Ordnance Committee recommended the design's standardization as the 'M4 Medium Tank'. That recommendation, along with a couple of modifications to the vehicle's machine-gun armament, received final approval from the US Army in October 1941.

Construction of pre-production pilot examples of the M4 for Ordnance Department approval began in November 1941. The following month the decision was made that the initial designation would be reserved only for those M4s built with a welded RHA upper hull. Those with the CHA upper hull received the designation M4A1 Medium Tank.

The Ordnance Committee

In the official US Army history of the Second World War, in the volume titled *The Ordnance Department: Planning Munitions for War* is an explanation of the function of the Ordnance Committee, which eventually became the Ordnance Technical Committee:

> After March 1942, the Army Ground Forces [AGF] ... spoke for the combat arms. But the user had the final say about what would be acceptable to him. Sometimes one desired feature ruled out another; maneuverability and high road speed in a tank might preclude use of heavy armor plate or powerful guns. What was essential for the Infantry might be unimportant for the Cavalry and vice versa. Hence decisions as to what was of primary importance, what of secondary, were often hard to reach. These questions were resolved by the Ordnance Committee, composed of members of the Ordnance Department and the using services.
>
> When the principal 'military characteristics' were agreed upon in the Ordnance Committee, the Ordnance Department worked out a design, built a pilot model and subjected it to tests. The using arms studied its performance, suggested, if need be, modifications and later scrutinized the resulting modified weapon. If that appeared to be acceptable, the Ordnance Department made a limited number for test under service conditions.
>
> The using arm conducted the final service test. Only when both using arm and Ordnance designers concurred that the item was satisfactory in all essentials did the General Staff authorize the Ordnance Department to officially accept or 'standardize' it, and issue orders for quantity fabrication.

Until the spring of 1943, M4 Medium Tanks built by the Pressed Steel Car Company left the factory floor with riveted RHA lower hulls. After that, they came with welded RHA lower hulls. The M4A1 Medium Tank, along with all the other models of the tank, rolled off the factory floors with welded RHA lower hulls. Both the M4 and M4A1 Medium Tanks weighed around 33 tons.

Among M4-series tankers, there was some debate on what type of upper-hull armor provided superior protection: CHA or welded RHA. Post-war testing by the US Army concluded that welded RHA provided a higher level of protection from projectile strikes.

Engines

The M4 and M4A1 received power from the same gasoline-powered, air-cooled, radial engine. From a report titled *Summary of Lesson Learned in Combat*, Headquarters 1st Armored Group, dated November 1944, is the following extract: 'The M4 tank has proved itself very reliable mechanically. Our tanks traveled some 1,200 miles between 15 August and 15 October [1944], with relatively few mechanical failures.'

Some American tankers thought a bit less of the M4's radial engines. In a March 1945 report titled *United States vs. German Equipment* is this quote by Technical Sergeant William Schaning: 'Our old M4 and M4A1 with the radial-type motor did not have enough power, were too slow in low gears to give maneuverability, not dependable, and now we are receiving rebuilt Continental [radial engines] that sometimes will only run a few hours without causing trouble.'

In an immediate post-war research report prepared for the Armored School and titled *Armor on Luzon* there appears the following passage:

The M4 and M4A1 tanks with which the battalion was equipped were definitely underpowered for operations in support of infantry on such difficult terrain. In order to ascend a number of slopes, it was necessary to tow the tanks by tractors or to slip the clutch and jump the tank forward.

Other Design Features

Other versions, with different engine arrangements, were standardized as the M4A2, M4A3, M4A4 and M4A6. All first-generation M4-series tanks came off the production line with the same CHA turret armed with the same 75mm Gun M3.

The M4A2, M4A3, M4A4 and M4A6 all featured many small and sometimes large differences in design from the original M4 and M4A1, as well as from each other. The differences reflected the factory from which each came shortages of major components, and when they were manufactured, as there were continuing refinements made to answer user feedback and to speed up production.

Initially the first-generation M4-series CHA turret design included a removable front plate that could have accepted one of five different weapon combinations besides the 75mm Gun M3. Examples included three .50 caliber machine guns for the anti-aircraft role, a 105mm howitzer with a coaxial .30 caliber machine gun and a British Army 6-pounder (57mm) gun and a coaxial .30 caliber machine gun.

Improving Flotation

During the Italian campaign, operations in the MTO proved challenging for the first-generation M4 Sherman tanks with the VVSS due to Italy's often inclement weather conditions, poor transportation network and rugged terrain. From a post-war Armored School research report titled *Maintenance of Armor in World War II* is this description of the problems mud could pose:

> The tanks experienced great difficulty in the marshland, for the river had been dammed and diverted, with the result that twenty-six tanks were bogged down in the area between the river and the road ... Six tanks eventually crossed the river; of these, four were lost on mines or knocked out by concealed SP [self-propelled] guns, and the remaining two ran short of ammunition and were forced to return. In the meantime, the battalion commander and his executive officer got twenty-five more tanks across at two other crossings. The enemy had towed up a 75mm AT [anti-tank] gun, which set upon the tanks bogged in the marshes.

To improve the off-road mobility, by lowering the ground pressure of those Sherman tanks fitted with VVSS, in 1944 the Ordnance Department designed 'extended end connectors' that attached to the outside edge of tank tracks. Unofficial nicknames for these included 'duckbills', 'duck feet' and 'paddle wheels'.

Captain Henry W. Johnson, 2nd Armored Division, stated in the *United States vs. German Equipment Report* of March 1945 his opinion on extended end connectors:

> The field expedient of duckbills added to widen the Sherman tread aids but does not affect the advantage the German Mark V [Panther] and Mark VI [Tiger] have. It is my opinion that the Mark V and Mark VI Tiger enemy tank is far superior in maneuverability to our own Sherman tanks.

M4 and M4A1

American factories and arsenals would build a total of 6,748 examples of the M4 Medium Tank starting in July 1942 and ending in January 1944. They manufactured another 6,281 examples of the M4A1 Medium Tank, starting in February 1942 and concluding in January 1944.

The M4 and M4A1 would form the mainstay of the US Army's first-generation medium tank inventory during the Second World War. A small number of M4A1s would also see service with the Marine Corps beginning in 1943.

Under Lend-Lease, the British Army received 2,096 examples of the M4 and 942 examples of the M4A1. A single M4A1 had been shipped to the British 8th Army in North Africa, arriving in August 1942. It was to be followed by more significant numbers over the following months, consisting mostly of M4A1s with a few M4A2s included.

The British 8th Army first employed its new American-supplied Sherman tanks in combat in October 1942. They would eventually become the most numerous tanks with the British Army in that theater and for the remainder of the Second World War. The British Army would later transfer some of them to its Commonwealth armies.

Composite Hull M4

Of the 6,748 examples of the M4 built, 1,418 came with the front upper hull of an M4A1 welded on in place of the original welded RHA arrangement. The non-official label for the arrangement was 'composite'. M4 tanks with the composite configuration became the 'Sherman I Hybrid' in British Army service.

The reason behind the composite combination revolved around the fact that CHA sections were more cost-effective and quicker to make than a corresponding welded RHA section, especially the complex glacis of a Sherman tank.

The builders of the composite tanks officially listed them as the M4 Medium Tank, as did the US Army, although in a few test reports they were referred to as M4A1s by mistake. The composite vehicles came off the assembly lines between August 1943 and January 1944. Early production examples had the original narrow overhead hatches for the driver and bow gunner, with later production vehicles having new larger overhead hatches for those crew positions.

M4A2

Due to the wartime shortage of gasoline-powered, air-cooled, radial engines, as aircraft had a higher priority for these engines, the Ordnance Department put the same twin-diesel-engine arrangement they had installed in the M3A2 and M3A3 Medium Tanks into the M4A2 Medium Tank. Testing confirmed that the twin-diesel-engine arrangement in the M4A2 was superior to the gasoline engines in the M4/M4A1, both in performance and reliability.

Of the six versions of the Sherman, the M4A2 model proved to be the most numerous, with 8,053 examples completed between April 1942 and May 1944. The War Department announced in March 1942 that only gasoline-engine-powered tanks be shipped overseas with the US Army. As a result, the majority of M4A2 tanks were allocated to Lend-Lease.

The British Army received 5,041 examples of the M4A2 through Lend-Lease. They considered it the best of the first-generation Sherman tanks due to its superior speed, range and overall mechanical reliability compared to those powered by gasoline radial engines. Through Lend-Lease, the Red Army received 1,990 examples of the M4A2. An additional 382 examples went off to other Allied armies, such as the Free French, under Lend-Lease.

In 1943 the US Marine Corps received 168 M4A2 tanks as there were no other Sherman models available. The Marines were reluctant at first to accept them, as many Marine tankers regarded them as 'stinkers'. However, when combat experience demonstrated that they were less likely to catch fire from enemy anti-tank weapons due to diesel fuel being far less flammable than gasoline, Marine tankers heartily embraced them.

M4A3

The partial late-war replacement for the M4 and M4A1 in the US Army would be the M4A3 Medium Tank, with 1,690 examples built between June 1942 and September 1943. It had a welded RHA hull, like the M4. Its main difference was its water-cooled, gasoline-powered engine, labeled the Ford GAA. The Ford engine proved superior to the gasoline-powered, air-cooled, radial engines of the M4 and M4A1.

Pictorial evidence seems to indicate that none of the first-generation M4A3s made it to the MTO, with only a few images showing remanufactured examples appearing in the ETO by 1945. The majority built must have been employed as training tanks in the United States. The British Army received only seven examples of the first-generation M4A3 under Lend-Lease and never used them in combat.

M4A4

The second most numerous Sherman tank built bore the designation M4A4. A total of 7,499 examples came off the factory floor between July 1942 and September 1943. Like the M3A4, the M4A4 received power from five Chrysler liquid-cooled, gasoline truck engines coupled together, labeled the A-57 Multibank. Due to the size of this engine arrangement, the M4A4 had to have its hull lengthened.

Despite being gasoline-powered, the US Army wanted nothing to do with the M4A4 and its complex engine arrangement, seeing only a maintenance nightmare. US Army testing of the M4A4 confirmed that the A-57 Multibank proved the least satisfactory of the engines in the Sherman series. As a result, the Army decided not to use the tank overseas. A few did see use as training tanks in the United States, with twenty-two going to the Marine Corps, which never used them in combat.

With the US Army's rejection of the M4A4, the vehicle became available for Lend-Lease, with the British Army receiving 7,167 examples and some 274 going to the Free French Army. The US Army's poor opinion of the

A-57 Multibank engine was seconded by the British Army when they had their first chance to see the engine arrangement. However, with a heavy emphasis on maintenance, the British Army found that the M4A4 performed adequately for their needs, as the individual engines were very reliable and, like the twin-diesel arrangement, provided powerplant redundancy, albeit at a lower level of performance.

During the Battle of the Bulge (December 1944 to January 1945), the British Army transferred 351 of its Lend-Lease Sherman tanks to the US Army to make up for heavy losses among US Army armored units. These included the M4A4. A US Army report stated that, unfortunately, the British-supplied M4A4s did not come with any spare parts.

M4A6

The Ordnance Committee made a continuing effort to find other engines for the Sherman. In response, the Caterpillar Tractor Company came up with an air-cooled, radial engine that could operate on a variety of petroleum products, including gasoline and diesel fuel. The new multi-fuel engine received the designation RD1820.

Promising results with the RD1820 led to a decision that would involve having 775 examples of the M4A4 fitted with the Caterpillar engine while on the production line. The modified M4A4s would be assigned the designation M4A6. The first example left the factory floor in October 1943.

Changing requirements led to the cancelation of the M4A6 in February 1944 after only seventy-five examples of the vehicle had been completed. One of the factors contributing to the demise of the M4A6 revolved around the US Army's preference for the M4A3. All the M4A6s built were in the composite configuration, with a welded RHA upper rear hull welded to a CHA front upper hull.

Despite cancellation of the M4A6, the US Army went ahead and tested ten of the vehicles beginning in March 1944. Results demonstrated that the RD1820 offered the highest level of performance compared to any of the other engine arrangements in the first-generation Sherman tanks. None of the M4A6s went overseas; all remained in the United States as training vehicles.

Into the Fray

The first British Army Sherman tanks saw combat during the Second Battle of El Alamein (October 23, 1942 until November 1942). The British tankers proved very enthusiastic about their new tanks as they possessed superior firepower to their British counterparts, and they presented a lower profile than the M3 Medium Tank series. As of December 1944, the

British Army had obtained through Lend-Lease a total of 15,153 examples of the first-generation Sherman tanks armed with a 75mm gun.

The Sherman tanks in US Army use generally did not fare well in North Africa (November 1942 till May 1943), due primarily to poor leadership and faulty doctrine. That doctrine insisted that towed anti-tank guns or self-propelled tank destroyers deal with enemy tanks. Time after time, the typically inexperienced and overly confident American tankers charged combat-experienced German combined arms formations and were almost always severely mauled.

In the July 1943 report *Tankers in Tunisia*, Lieutenant Colonel Louis V. Hightower of the 1st Armored Division stated:

> Four 88mm guns, if dug in, are a match for any tank company [seventeen tanks]. They are the most wonderful things to camouflage I have ever seen. They are very low to the ground. You can watch the fire coming in, little dust balls on the ground give them away and show how low they are.

The British Army tankers had tried to warn the US Army tankers about the German anti-tank gun traps and the painful lessons they had learned in fighting the German Army in North Africa. However, in their unreserved arrogance, the Americans looked down upon their British Army allies as inferior, despite their accumulated combat experience.

First-Hand Experience

An early post-war report, prepared by Captain Charles L. Davis for the Academic Department of the Infantry School, recounted his impressions of a battle he observed on May 6, 1943 against a German defensive position near Mateur, Tunisia. It involved a tank battalion of the

1st Armored Division, equipped with Sherman tanks, which he considered under-gunned and under-armored:

> Almost simultaneously the battlefield erupted into action, characterized by flashes from anti-tank guns sending out their screaming red, high-velocity projectiles in a crisscross pattern, and the almost steady flame of the high cyclic rate machine guns pouring streams of tracers onto the tanks as they started to burn ... The seven tanks burning in front of the position, in addition to the seven fire-blacked hulls lost by the 3rd Battalion the day before, were grim reminders of the terrific power and devastating effect of the German anti-tank guns. Every time a round of 75mm ammunition exploded inside a tank, the burning tank belched black smoke rings toward the sky, and the fragments could be heard rattling around inside.

Opinions on the Sherman

During testimony by General Levin H. Campbell, Chief of the Ordnance Department, before Congress on May 9, 1943, he stated that 'They [the Sherman tanks] overcame every tank which they opposed.' The Axis forces in North Africa surrendered on May 13, 1943.

In the July 1943 report titled *Tankers in Tunisia*, US Army Brigadier General T.J. Camp recounted that a British officer with tank experience in North Africa told him ' ... our M4 was the finest tank in the world, and better than anything the Germans had.' With a bit of hyperbole, the same British officer went on to say: 'He thought it [M4] would be the best tank for the next five years.'

Dissenting Opinions

In his 1951 autobiography titled *A Soldier's Story*, General Omar N. Bradley wrote the following:

> When I asked about our equipment, I learned that our gasoline-driven Shermans had already established a bad reputation among US troops at the front [North Africa] ... In their first engagement, the American tankers learned that tank-for-tank their General Grants [Lees] and Shermans were no match for the more heavily-armored and better-gunned German panzers Mark IV.

Brigadier General Paul M. Robinett of the 1st Armored Division, during the North African campaign, wrote in his 1958 autobiography *Armored Command* that American tanks were not on a par with German tanks. He would go on to state in his book:

> During the war, there was a pronounced tendency to cover up our deficiencies by propagandistic statements to the effect that American tanks were the best in the world. It is worse than useless to try to convince a soldier that his weapons are the best in the world when his experience tells him otherwise.

From the official history of the US Army in the Second World War, in the volume titled *The Ordnance Department: Procurement and Supply* it is noted that the public acclaim lavished upon American tanks was offset by

> the secret reports on tank performance submitted by overseas commanders (both American and British) and the Armored Force Board told a somewhat different story. Along with frequent words of praise came many complaints, ranging from the lack of good binoculars to the inferiority of US tanks and armor to the German guns and armor pitted against them.

Sherman Issues

A sergeant from the 1st Armored Division, quoted in the 1943 *Tankers in Tunisia* report, stated that after being burned out of two gasoline-engine-powered Sherman tanks, he concluded that he would prefer having a diesel-engine-powered Sherman tank. He perceived it as less likely to catch fire upon penetration by enemy projectiles.

The sergeant's opinion found support in a memo submitted on March 1, 1943 by Colonel Stanley J. Grogan to another Army officer. The memo, *Recap of Pertinent Issues from Interviews with Personnel of the 1st Armored Division*, stated that many American tankers preferred diesel-engine-powered Sherman tanks.

Major General Ernest N. Harmon, stated in a March 2, 1943 memo to Lieutenant General Jacob L. Devers, commander of the Armored Force:

I wish our tanks were diesel-operated instead of gas. Practically all of our tanks that are hit catch on fire, which is caused by the high-velocity [German] 75mm, which is red hot, igniting the leaking gasoline which comes from ruptured tanks when the vehicle is hit. This is a very serious morale factor, and the men want diesels.

In the 1943 *Tankers in Tunisia* report, Lieutenant Colonel Louis V. Hightower of the 1st Armored Division had this opinion on what caused his Sherman tanks to catch fire:

Our losses were from burning gasoline. Shells seemed to end up in the gas tank invariably. The projectile goes streaking through the whole tank dragging the gasoline out with it, and the first thing you know, the whole thing is aflame. It burns very fast. They hit my tank six times before they got the gas. An 88 shell went in right behind the left rear bogie and hit the gas tank.

We find the same thought in a passage from an After-Action Report of Combat Command A (CCA) of the 2nd Armored Division, concerning operations conducted between April 21 and July 25, 1943 in Sicily. In it, an officer states: 'I think diesel is the best-fireproofing material. I had ten diesel-driven tanks for range firing at Fort Bragg. Unless supply problems prevent, I don't see why we haven't standardized on diesels.' Another officer in the same report stated: 'I believe the gasoline-diesel controversy can be better settled on the proving ground than on the battlefield.'

The Answer

To address the perceived issue of gasoline-engine-powered Sherman tanks being more susceptible to burning than their diesel-engine-powered counterparts, a series of tests took place in the United States. These tests demonstrated that it was not the fuel but the main gun ammunition propellant fires that were the main culprit of catastrophic kills.

In March 21, 1950, in a US Army Report titled *The Vulnerability of Armored Vehicles to Ballistic Attack* was the following extract:

At least as early as 1942 it was realized that the ammunition stored in combat vehicles constituted a serious hazard to the crew and the vehicles themselves ... Practically all ammunition fires caused by penetrating projectiles start within a few seconds and, in most cases, before the crew can evacuate. In many cases, the crew is dazed after a direct hit and are unable to leave the vehicle immediately.

Design Shortcomings

The reason for the ammunition propellant fires in first-generation Sherman tanks (be they gasoline- or diesel-powered) was twofold:

1. The German tanks' AP projectiles had an HE filler. The filler would explode after penetrating a tank's armor and detonate the unprotected main gun rounds contained within. (American 75mm AP ammunition had no HE filler until late in the Second World War.)
2. Most of the main gun rounds in early-production Sherman tanks were stored horizontally on either side of the vehicle's upper hull; areas referred to as sponsons. The rounds stored there were in non-armored metal bins. Twelve main gun rounds were also stored vertically within the confines of the tank's turret and held in place by metal clips.

An unnamed British Army officer quoted in the *Tankers in Tunisia* report believed that the German gunners were deliberately targeting the sponsons of first-generation Sherman tanks to improve their odds of destroying the vehicles. He stated: 'In one battalion 15 tanks were penetrated; 11 of them burned, 10 because of ammunition … In another battle, 15 tanks were penetrated; 7 burned, all but one by ammunition fires.'

Protection

The thickest armor on the first generation of Sherman tanks was the 89mm (3.5in) on their turret gun shields, except for the early-production examples that were 76mm (3in) thick. The front of the turret was also 76mm (3in) thick, and the sides 51mm (2in) thick. With the addition of a narrow 51mm (2in) thick rotor shield on the early-production vehicles, Sherman armor thickness came out to 127mm (5in).

Both the frontal armor of the tank's upper hull and lower hull were 51mm (2in) thick. Like the M3 series, the Sherman was supposed to offer frontal protection from the German towed 37mm anti-tank gun as well as artillery fire. There was 13mm (0.5in) of armor on the rear upper hull and lower hull.

At the front of the Sherman tank, the hull floor came in at 25mm (1in) thick, decreasing to 13mm (0.5in) at the rearward portion of the lower hull floor. Although the German Army did make use of anti-tank mines, according to Allied reports they did not seem to cause many crew casualties.

German Tanks Did Not Burn

In a March 1943 document by the 2nd Armored Division titled *Report of Visit to the Tunisian Front*, there appears an interesting passage that may have had something to do with the lack of an HE filler in the 75mm main gun AP rounds: 'Practically all of our tanks that are hit are thoroughly destroyed by burning. This is a matter which should receive very serious consideration, as it has been noted that German tanks that have been hit do not burn, and are apparently very easily and promptly recovered.'

From a British Army report listed as the *Work of No. 2 Operational Research Section with the 21st Army Group, June 1944 to July 1945*, is the following brief passage:

> From Table VIII it would appear that the percentage of brew-ups for the Panther (Pz Kw Mk V) is materially less than that for the Sherman. Too much importance, however, must not be attached to this difference by itself since British and German gunners may differ in their tendencies to fire.

In a quote from a March 1, 1951 report titled a *Survey of Allied Tank Casualties in World War II* is this extract: 'The American tank appears to be more susceptible to fire when hit than the German.' All German tanks were gasoline-engine-powered. The propensity of American tanks to burn and German tanks not to burn lent the Germans a tremendous advantage, assuming they could recover damaged vehicles from the battlefield.

Why Not Thicker Armor?

The decision to not design the first-generation Sherman tanks with thicker armor was based on several reasons. These included the Army's desire for a highly mobile vehicle, something not possible with heavier armor due to the limited automotive performance of the engines then available.

Lieutenant General Lesley J. McNair, commander of the Army Ground Forces (AGF) and the second most powerful man in the US Army, attached a great deal of importance to the ease with which tanks could be shipped overseas. This, in turn, heavily influenced both their size and weight. The Sherman designers found themselves restricted by the lifting capacity of ships' cranes and the load-carrying capacity of the Army's then in-service portable bridges, as well as their width limits.

Another issue was the Ordnance Department's failure to anticipate the continuing trend of bore-size increase in German tank main guns and towed or mechanized anti-tank guns. The German 37mm towed anti-tank gun, introduced into service in 1936, was superseded by a towed 50mm anti-tank gun in 1941, which in turn was replaced by a 7.5cm (75mm) towed anti-tank gun Pak 40 in 1942 and the 8.8cm (88mm) Pak 43 in 1943.

Surveys of Tank Losses

A report by the American First Army listing tank losses (both light and medium) in the ETO between June 1944 and April 1945 indicates a total of 898 destroyed, with 502 attributed to gunfire. The others included 171 to mines, 119 to enemy hand-held anti-tank weapons (*panzerfausts* and *panzershrecks*) and 106 to unknown causes.

A US Army report dated June 6, 1945 titled *Observations on Problems in Armored Units* stated that from 60 to 90 percent of first-generation Sherman tanks caught fire and burned after being struck by enemy anti-tank guns and almost all when hit by German hand-held anti-tank weapons. A post-war US Army report 'indicated that from 90 to 95 percent of all non-repairable tanks in World War II were burned out. Practically all of these were from ammunition fires.' It's important to note that a significant fire destroys a tank's armor's resistance to penetration, thus a tank that burned would be a total write-off.

In an Operation Research Office paper titled a *Survey of Allied Tank Casualties in World War II* there is a breakdown of 1,082 tank losses (both light and medium) in the ETO. A total of 394 burned, 300 of which were due to anti-tank guns, with the remaining 94 burning due to enemy hand-held anti-tank weapons, mines and mortar fire. Of those tanks that did not burn, more than half suffered penetrations by anti-tank guns, the others by the other weapons already mentioned.

Sherman tanks that were penetrated but did not burn would often go off for repair. From a post-war Armored School research report titled *Maintenance of Armor in World War II*: 'From the time the 3rd Armored Division started in action (June 29, 1944) to 21 Sept. 1944, 436 medium tanks were knocked out by enemy action. Of this amount, 200 were repaired by the division and put back into service.'

Tank Crew Losses

An American First Army report that reviewed casualties for both light and medium tanks in the ETO identified which crew position on tanks suffered the worst losses from penetration (and the after-effects). It determined casualties were somewhat evenly distributed among crewmen, taking into account the M5 light tank series had four-man crews rather than the five-man crews of the Sherman tank.

In a post-war Operation Research Office paper titled a *Survey of Allied Tank Casualties in World War II* is the following extract: 'Penetrations of the tank by AT projectiles usually results in...about two casualties, one killed and one wounded.' The report went on to state:

> When complete crews are lost, unit's CO's attribute casualties to flash ammunition fires which spring up so rapidly that wounded or shocked members cannot evacuate themselves or be evacuated before overcome by flame. Also, it is believed that in a number of cases, exits may have been blocked by wounded members of the crew and thus preventing escape of other members.

Get Out Fast

The fear of burning alive in a Sherman affected all tank crewmen. James Carroll, a Marine Corps tank commander on Iwo Jima, recalled in a 2006 interview that nobody had to be told to bail out of their tanks when struck. On one occasion, he recalled that when something hit the tank, his gunner somehow managed to crawl over him to get out of the tank before he did by way of the commander's cupola.

Tom Sator, a Sherman loader of the 4th Armored Division, recalled in a 2006 interview that when the officers were not around, he and his fellow tankers referred to their tanks as 'flaming coffins'. Jim Francis, a Sherman tank gunner in the 5th Armored Division, recalled in a 2006 interview that he and his fellow tankers called their tanks 'steel coffins' and many other morbid nicknames.

In an early 1944 story by *New York Times* correspondent Cyrus Sulzberger that was quashed by the US Army's senior leadership, the writer quoted two colonels he interviewed in Italy about a battle planned for the next day: 'There will be plenty of flamers. Germans have been able to make this sector a regular trap, and we haven't got guns to stand up against them.' Note the pejorative term 'flamers'.

The Sherman Tank's Intended Role

The first-generation Sherman tanks, armed with their 75mm main gun, were not envisioned as tank killers by US Army leadership. Their primary role was as a weapon of 'exploitation', a doctrinal concept conceived and promoted by the powerful Cavalry Branch of the US Army. They, rather than the Infantry Branch, took on the reins of the newly-formed Armored Force in June 1940 and began to dictate doctrine.

For the exploitation role favored by the Cavalry Branch, the tank's designers placed mobility above protection and firepower in importance.

Mobility, by default, also meant that a tank had to be both reliable and durable, which would stand the Sherman tank in good stead through the Second World War.

A US Army Armored Force manual, dated March 7, 1942, stated that 'offensive operations of armored units, acting either alone or as part of a combined force, are characterized by rapid thrusts into vital parts of the hostile rear followed by immediate exploitation to complete enemy demoralization.'

Patton, in his *Letters of Instruction No. 2* issued on April 3, 1944 to the corps and divisional commanders of the Third Army, stated: 'The primary mission of armored units is the attacking of infantry and artillery. The enemy's rear is the happy hunting ground for armor; use every means to get it there.'

How Exploitation was Supposed to Work

Exploitation, as envisioned by a pre-war US Army, involved infantry divisions, supported by artillery and aircraft, breaking through German front-line. Once accomplished, armored divisions would advance through the gap created in the German lines.

When in the enemy's rear areas, the Sherman was to destroy artillery positions, command and control nodes, and other rear-echelon units, primarily with machine-gun fire, according to an April 22, 1943 manual entitled *Tank Gunnery*.

Doctrine stressed that it would be doubtful if enemy tanks appeared in their rear areas. However, if encountered, a passage from a March 1942 manual titled *Tactics and Technique* described the appropriate actions to be taken in such an event: 'Against equal or superior hostile armored forces, friendly armored units will avoid frontal assault and maneuver to cut off or destroy armored units' supply facilities, followed by blows against the rear of enemy detachments.' Unfortunately, tactical and terrain conditions typically made this maneuver very difficult. The 2nd Armored Division's tank battalion commanders claimed it proved impossible to perform their assigned missions without having to engage enemy tanks.

New Opinions on the Sherman

In a March 18, 1945 letter to the commanding general of the 2nd Armored Division, General Isaac White, General Dwight D. Eisenhower, Supreme Commander of the Allied Expeditionary Forces in Europe (SHAEF), solicited his opinion, and that of his men, on American tanks, as well as other military equipment, compared to their German counterparts. Those findings appeared in a March 27, 1945 report titled *United States versus German Equipment*.

In his letter to White, based on his conversations with junior officers and enlisted men of armored units, General Eisenhower wrote: 'Our men, in general, realize that the Sherman is not capable of standing up in a ding-dong, head-on fight with a Panther. Neither in gun power nor in armor is the present Sherman justified in undertaking such a contest.'

Lieutenant General John H. Collier of the 2nd Armored Division responded in the report Eisenhower requested with the following statement: 'The fact that our equipment must be shipped over long distances does not, in the opinion of our tankers, justify our inferiority.' In the same report, Lieutenant Colonel Wilson M. Hawkins stated: 'We have been outgunned since Tunisia when the Germans brought out their Mark IV Special [Mark IV Ausf. F/G] with the long-barreled 75mm gun.'

The enlisted men of the 2nd Armored Division also voiced their opinions. Tank commander Sergeant Moore and his crew commented:

> As we go now every man has resigned himself to dying sooner or later because we don't have a chance against the German tanks. All this stuff that we read about German tanks knocked out by our tanks makes us sick because we know what prices we have to pay in men and equipment to accomplish this.

More Opinions

Eisenhower also sent a letter on March 18, 1945 to Major General Maurice Rose, commander of the 3rd Armored Division, asking for his opinion and that of his men, comparing American and German equipment. Rose wrote back to Eisenhower in a March 21, 1945 letter in which he stated: 'It is my personal conviction that the present M4A3 tank is inferior to the German Mark V [Panther].' He went on to say that his men made up for their 'inferior equipment by the efficient use of artillery, air support and maneuver'.

Staff Sergeant Robert M. Early, a tank commander in the 3rd Armored Division, stated in the same 3rd Armored Division report: 'I haven't any confidence in an M4. Jerry armament will knock out an M4 as far as they can see it.'

Wolfgang Sterner, Panther tank commander in the Panzer Lehr Division, recalled in a 2003 interview that he thought little of the American Sherman tanks as they were easy to destroy. However, once engaged, the Sherman tanks would fire smoke rounds and withdraw. It was the artillery-spotter planes he feared. Once they arrived overhead, it meant a storm of artillery or an appearance by fighter-bombers in short order.

Panther Kills Five Sherman Tanks

In a 2014 interview, Brigadier General Albin F. Irzyk (ret.), a battalion commander in the 4th Armored Division during the Second World War, recalled something he saw in the hedgerows of France in July 1944, reflecting on the training (or lack thereof) of US Army tankers:

> I was roaming around and saw this knocked-out Panther tank. I went to it, got up on the back, and lo and behold I looked down the barrel and saw these five American tanks. Whoever the platoon leader was had zero training because he did everything he should not have done. First, the five tanks were in a row. We taught them to stagger the tanks and not to be at the same range. So, if we had a German gunner, he's not going to go 'boom, boom' – which he did then [rapid destruction of one tank after another]. If you spread your tanks in an irregular formation, the German gunner must aim at each one separately, different range, different distance. But this platoon was advancing five in a row, and as big as you could possibly see was this white star [national identification painted on the front hull on American tanks]. And there was the shot. All he [the German tank gunner] had to do was 'bang, bang, bang'. It was like Coney Island.

On those wartime occasions when German lines collapsed, the Sherman tank lived up to the US Army's expectation as a vehicle of exploitation, such as in pursuit of a demoralized enemy over long distances. Examples include France, August to September 1944, and the waning months of the war, in the ETO, from February to May 1945.

How Often

In a March 1, 1951 Operations Research Office paper by John Hopkins University titled a *Survey of Allied Tank Casualties in World War II* is this extract confirming that tank-on-tank encounters were relatively rare for the Sherman in all theaters:

> ... US Armor in World War II seems never to have devoted itself to fighting enemy armor in more than one out of four engagements. The overall percentage of tank vs. tank, as a ratio of total targets, averaged about 15 percent. Buildings, fortifications and personnel each seem to have attracted the greater attention of the tank.

The lack of tank-on-tank engagements in the ETO is also apparent in the fact that most main gun rounds fired by Sherman tanks were HE and not

AP. This was true of all the various theaters in which tanks participated during the Second World War. White phosphorous (smoke rounds) constituted about 10 percent of the main gun rounds fired by Sherman tanks.

According to US Army post-war studies in reviewing tank-versus-tank fighting in the ETO, the typical engagement involved no more than a combined total of thirteen tanks. A US Army report titled *Armor vs. Mud and Mines* subtitled '4th Armored Division in the Saar-Moselle Area' contains this passage on one reason why German tanks typically operated in small groups. From the commanding general of the 11th Panzer Division: 'In view of the enemy supremacy in the air, we had to attack with small tank detachments. [German] Speed, flexibility and surprise had to make good the [American] numerical and material superiority.'

The US Army's 2nd Armored Division's most significant tank-on-tank engagement in the ETO involved approximately twenty-five German tanks and took place on November 17, 1944 outside Puffendorf, Germany. During the engagement, two of the 2nd Armored's tank battalions found themselves riddled at long range by Panthers and Tigers, losing thirty-eight medium tanks and nineteen light tanks for the loss of only five Panthers.

German Tank Gun Sights

An explanation for German tank gun accuracy at longer ranges appears in the March 1945 report titled *United States vs. German Equipment*. It comes from gunner Howard A. Wood: 'The German sights are better than ours, as they are able to choose their power between 2 and 6-power, where ours is a stationary 3-power. The German sights have lighted graduations and can lay on a target at night.'

In the same 2nd Armored Division report, tank commander J.C. Baker stated: 'For shooting into the sun they just flip a lever which just lets down a colored lens, reducing the glare.'

Sergeant Moninnis and crew of the 2nd Armored Division stated: 'As for the sights, our gunner has very much more vision than the German, but we have seen our tanks knocked out from ranges as far as 2,000 and 3,000 yards.'

The Sherman tank in later models had both a telescopic gun sight with a very narrow field of view and a periscopic gun sight with a much wider field of view. The German tanks had only a telescopic gun sight, but they sometimes supplemented this with range-finders borrowed from anti-aircraft units to take advantage of the long-range accuracy and power of the Panther and Tiger cannons.

Engaging Enemy Tanks

For first-generation Sherman tanks designed for the exploitation role, the 15 percent of the time spent engaging enemy tanks could be a severe problem due in large part to German tank designers optimizing their tanks as tank-killers. This doctrinal change began in 1942 based on their combat experiences fighting the Red Army's tanks.

From the After-Action Report of CCA of the 2nd Armored Division covering the period between April 21 and July 25, 1943 an officer commented: 'We destroyed Mark VIs [Tiger I tanks] with our 75mm guns on their suspensions, tracks and engine compartment, but no known penetration.'

An officer in the 191st Tank Battalion would write in an August 1944 report that his unit's 75mm armed Sherman tanks were no match for any German tanks. He would go on to state: 'This situation has a tremendous effect on the morale of the tank crews. This was evidenced by the reluctance of crews to fire on German tanks, feeling that it would do no good and would result in their being promptly knocked out.'

From the report titled *United States vs. German Equipment*, Sherman tank gunner Howard A. Wood stated that his 75mm AP rounds bounced off the frontal armor of two Panther tanks at a distance of less than 400 yards. In the same report, Francis W. Baker, a tank commander, expressed his disgust when his gunner put seven rounds into the supposedly thinner side armor of a Panther tank at a distance of 800 yards, all of them bouncing off.

The M61 APC round fired by the Sherman tank's 75mm Gun M3 could not penetrate the frontal hull armor on late-war Mark IV medium tanks at normal combat ranges. It could, however, penetrate the frontal turret armor of the German tank at normal combat ranges. The more potent 75mm gun on the late-war Mark IV tanks could penetrate both the frontal armor on the Sherman tank's turret and hull at normal combat ranges. Thus, a hull-down Sherman in a defensive position had rough parity, but an advancing Sherman with its hull exposed was at a disadvantage.

Heavy Losses

In the US Army's official multi-volume history of the Second World War, a passage from the volume titled *On Beachhead and Battlefront* describes the losses incurred by one US Army tank battalion in their efforts to take on the German armor from the sides or rear: '... between 26 July and 12 August, for example, one of 2nd Armored Division's tank battalions had lost to German tanks and assault guns 51 percent of its combat personnel killed or wounded and 70 percent of its tanks destroyed or evacuated for fourth-echelon repair.'

Tank commander Rains M. Robbins and driver Walter McGrail of the 2nd Armored Division stated in the March 1945 *United States vs. German Equipment* report: 'Since landing in France with this division, we've seen countless numbers of American tanks knocked out and burned with a resultant high loss of American lives, due, we believe, to our inferior tanks.' Most tankers knew that the infantry suffered much higher losses than they did in combat, but it is human nature to mainly be concerned about one's own situation.

Tom Sator, a 4th Armored Division tanker, recalled in a 2006 interview that he felt sorry for the infantry who hadn't any armor protection. He reconsidered that belief when an infantryman told Tom he felt sorry for him and other American tankers after seeing Sherman tanks burn with their crews.

The Closer, the Better

The Sherman's 75mm main gun stood a much better chance of destroying German tanks at very close ranges. Seen in a British Army report of tank actions that took place between June 27 and July 1, 1944 during the Battle for France is the following:

> [Lieutenant Fearn] saw his squadron commander engage a Tiger (previously examined by us). At 120 yards, the Tiger was head-on. The 75mm put three shots on it, and the crew bailed out without firing. He put in three more. The tank brewed up. Four shots had scooped on front plates, one had taken a piece out of the lower edge of the mantlet [gun shield], and gone into the tank through the roof, and one had ricocheted off the track into the sponson.

In a British Army report dated July 1, 1944 by 'C' Squadron of the 24th Lancers equipped with the first-generation Sherman tanks, an important lesson came into sharp focus: 'Do not engage Panthers when they are obviously out of 75mm range, no matter how tempting they appear. They are nearly always supported by Tigers or Panthers in concealed positions and are clearly put out to draw fire.'

Giving the Enemy a Bloody Nose

In September 1944, an eleven-day series of battles occurred near the French village of Arracourt between inexperienced German armored units equipped with the Panther tank and the battle-experienced US Army 4th Armored Division equipped with first-generation Sherman tanks. The

American tankers, aided by tank destroyers, badly bloodied their enemy counterparts, as dense ground fog rendered the German advantage in both long-range firepower and armor protection moot. The weather allowed the American first-generation 75mm gun tanks to engage the Panthers at very close ranges where their main guns could penetrate the German tanks' sides.

In the PTO

The Marine Corps invasion of Tarawa during November 20 to 23, 1943 was the first time the Sherman saw combat with the Corps. Due to the island's terrain and man-made obstacles, the tanks themselves proved of limited usefulness. However, they did contribute to the eventual seizure of the island.

In a post-war research report titled *Armor in Island Warfare* is an extract describing the fighting on the island of Betio in the Tarawa Atoll:

... the Marines moved into their final offensive to destroy the enemy's grip, with two Sherman tanks, the Colorado and China Gal ... As the Marines moved in, the Japanese in the biggest shelter suddenly broke from their cover and poured down the narrow exit channel. An infantry spotter rapped hard on the Colorado's side, and the tank commander swung his gun around and fired. It was [a] dream shot, point-blank, on the erupting stream of humanity. They estimated that fifty to seventy-five enemy troops were killed with this bowling-ball shot.

From the May 1950 *Armor in Island Warfare (Who, What and Where in the Pacific)* research report is this extract describing the type of fighting faced by US Army Sherman tankers:

As the lead tank rounded a sharp curve it was immediately hit by a round from an anti-tank gun. Orders were given to the second tank to back up out of the line of fire. In doing so, the driver accidentally backed off the road and the tank dropped about 400 feet. The third tank in the column was called up to give support while rescue efforts were made. As blood plasma was being given the wounded, the Japs counterattacked. They bayoneted the wounded. At the same time, two enemy tanks with explosives tied to them rounded a curve and rammed two of our tanks. A single man left in the tank loaded and fired the 75mm gun, knocking out the first enemy tank, and then assisted by the platoon leader knocked out the second one.

In another research report prepared for the Armored School and titled *Armor on Luzon*, appears this passage on Japanese tanks encountered:

All tanks were lightly armored with front plates and sides ranging from ¼ to 1 inch of armor. In actual combat, 75mm HE shells blew turrets off several tanks of the M95 [Type 95] series ... A 75mm AP projectile at a range of 100 to 500 yards entered the right front of a similar model and came out the rear ...

The same *Armor on Luzon* report mentioned that the US Army 710th Tank Battalion managed to develop an improvised canister round for its Sherman tanks. They combined a 75mm tank gun cartridge case with a canister projectile from a 75mm howitzer round. It proved very effective against Japanese positions on hillsides and in the brush at the crest of hills, according to the report.

Japanese Anti-Tank Defenses

The Japanese Army made productive use of its anti-tank assets when confronted by US Army and Marine Corps Sherman tanks. Although the Japanese Army's 37mm towed anti-tank guns had problems penetrating the medium tank's armor, this was not the case for its 47mm towed anti-tank gun, introduced into service in 1942.

An example of the 47mm anti-tank gun in action appears in this extract from a May 1945 Marine Corps 4th Division report on the 4th Tank

Battalion during the fighting on Iwo Jima: 'Anti-tank guns were generally of the standard 47mm types, but some large-caliber dual-purpose guns were encountered ... The 47mm had no difficulty penetrating [M4] tank armor except on the front slope Plate [*sic*] and the turret.'

For the Japanese Army, the last-ditch method of combating the Sherman relied on the bravery of its infantrymen. In an immediate post-war Research Report prepared for the Armored School titled *Armor on Okinawa* is this passage:

> The enemy groups, called 'satchel charge squads,' were teams of from three to nine men. Each man had a specific job. The first step was that of blinding the tank by the use of smoke grenades. To decrease the radius of vision of the tank the Japs forced the tank to button up by hurling fragmentation grenades. Then a 'yardstick' or 'tape measure' mine was placed under a track to immobilize the tank. The final touch was destruction of the tank (and crew) by placing a box mine under the tank. Attacks varied from carefully planned ambushes to fanatic charges across open ground toward the tanks.

By May of 1945, the fighting on Okinawa, involving five US Army tank battalions, had resulted in the loss of 221 tanks out of 338 on the island, the majority of which were Shermans. Of those lost, ninety-four were non-repairable. Of the 221 tanks lost in combat, enemy anti-tank guns accounted for almost half and mines another sixty-four, with the enemy's infantry tank-hunting teams knocking out or damaging twenty-five.

Stopgap Armoring of the Sherman

Beginning in the summer of 1943, additional armor plates were welded onto the upper hull and turret of first-generation Shermans to resolve potential ballistic weak spots that had been identified during the fighting in North Africa. These did not appear on later-production examples of the first-generation Sherman tanks, as the molds were thickened in those areas at the foundries.

To reduce the chance of detonation as a result of penetrating enemy anti-tank rounds, storage in the turret of the twelve vertical main gun rounds was ended. Armored bins replaced the unarmored main gun ammunition bins in the sponsons. These modifications began on the production lines around August 1943. Modification field kits under the 'Quick Fix' program were eventually shipped to England so that most of the Sherman tanks in the ETO had the same armor arrangement.

Unfortunately, the Quick Fix program did not apply to the Sherman tanks in the MTO (Italy), for whatever reason. The following is seen in a

1944 report titled *Trip to NATOUSA (North African Theater of Operations, US Army), Modifications of Medium Tanks*:

> The medium tanks in the theater are all of the old 1942 manufacture [M4 and M4A1]. They do not incorporate the modifications and corrections for deficiencies discovered in combat and testing in 1942 and 1943 ... Even when fully modified, these tanks will be greatly below the standard of 1944 production tanks.

More the Better

The Ordnance Department's efforts at increasing crew safety within first-generation Sherman tanks met with mixed feelings among tankers, as seen in this passage from the *Report of the New Weapon Board* dated April 27, 1944: 'There is no interest in further protection of ammunition if it would entail any decrease in the number of rounds carried. Ready racks in the turret are particularly desired, and the tank crews are extremely reluctant to give up the ready racks, even to increase safety.'

The dangerous habit of Sherman tank crews to overload their vehicles with ammunition when going into combat appears in a 1948 monograph. Titled *A Tank Company on Okinawa*: 'It is interesting to note that we stowed ammunition of all kinds in considerable excess to that specified in training manuals. Each tank carried fully 100 percent more .30 caliber ammunition than is specified and approximately 15 more rounds of 75mm.'

Some Sherman tank crews carried as many as forty extra main gun rounds when going into action. German tankers also tended to carry extra main gun ammunition in their vehicles, as did tankers of most nations, for fear of running short when in battle.

Reconnaissance by Fire

From Patton's *Letter of Instruction No. #3* issued on May 20, 1944 to his corps and divisional commanders:

> When tanks are advancing, they must use their guns for what is known as reconnaissance by fire; that is, they must shoot at any terrestrial objective behind which an anti-tank gun might be concealed and take these targets under fire at a range greater than that at which an anti-tank gun is effective; in other words, at a range greater than 2,000 yards. They should fire at these targets with high explosive or with white phosphorus, because if the enemy receives such fire, he will consider himself discovered and reply at a range so great as to render him ineffective.

As can be expected, those Sherman units who abided by the authorized main gun storage arrangements when penetrated by enemy anti-tank weapons suffered fewer vehicle burn-outs, resulting in fewer casualties.

In a US Army wartime document dated September 21, 1944, titled *Immediate Report No. 58* and subtitled 'Combat Observations' is the following extract: 'Tanks no longer take additional ammunition for the 75mm gun. The stowage provided has been found adequate, and the additional ammunition is subject to damage and dented cases, and reduces the efficiency of the crew.'

Armor Protection Issues

The actual protection provided by various armor upgrades at factories, or in the field, generally proved ineffective as most German high-velocity anti-tank weapons easily outmatched them with their penetration capabilities. An example of this outmatching appears in an extract from a wartime British Army document titled *Report No. 12 – Operational Research Section*, which addressed first-generation Sherman tank losses between June 6 and July 10, 1944 in Normandy, France:

> It should be recognized that in no recorded case in our sample has the extra outside appliqué armour resisted any hit ... The small number of AP hits failing to penetrate is noticeable. This small number has been confirmed by the opinions of technical adjutants, etc., who agree that the proportion was probably not above 5 per cent.

In the same report, there appears a passage from Sherman tank crews commenting on the poor quality of their vehicle's armor:

> There have also been complaints at the apparently low resisting power of the present Sherman armor. REME, 5 Gds Armoured Division state that an AP300 and an AP500 Browning, both fired at 100 yds range, penetrated ½ and 1½ inches respectively into the turret armor. Added to this, it is at present the practice to recondition for service partially brewed-up tanks whose quality of armor might often be low.

The problem with first-generation Sherman tanks' armor also appeared in the book titled *Mobility, Shock and Firepower: The Emergence of the US Army's Armor Branch, 1917–1945* written by Dr Robert S. Cameron, US Army Armor Branch historian and published by the US Army Center for Military History:

> Moreover, the quality of the M4 tank's armor initially proved inferior in its design. This flaw derived from the reliance of armor-plate

manufacturers on outdated armor-penetration data gathered from pre-war experiments with American tanks and anti-tank weapons. This data did not reflect the subsequent development of larger-caliber and higher-velocity anti-tank weapons or the parallel emergence of better anti-tank ammunition. Similarly, foreign achievements in these areas received scant attention. Only after combat revealed the inadequacies in American armor-plate design did changes begin to occur.

Improvised Armor in the ETO

As it became apparent to US Army Sherman tankers that their vehicles were under-armored, they quickly set about addressing the issue with whatever they could find, leading to a wide variety of improvised up-armored arrangements in both the ETO and the PTO. The makeshift armor included everything from inches of applied cement, welded-on track links and sandbags supported by welded-on metal brackets. Tests performed by various tank battalions led to the conclusion that the add-on concrete might not stop a tank from destruction by an enemy shaped-charge anti-tank weapon but did cut down on crew casualties.

Brigadier General Albin F. Irzyk of the 4th Armored Division, responding to a question in a 2014 interview regarding improvised protection applied to his tanks to defeat the shaped-charge *panzerfaust* threat, answered: 'One time during a brief period, I had my maintenance crew take concrete, additional armor and all sorts of things. They fired the *panzerfaust*, and it still went through. I said the heck with this.'

In a 1994 thesis written by US Army Major Matthew A. Boal titled *Field Expedient Armor Modifications to US Army Vehicles* and presented to the Faculty of the US Army Command and General Staff College is this passage on the sometime benefit of sandbagging M4 tanks:

> Sandbagging did significantly improve the overall effectiveness of armor against enemy weapons such as *panzerfausts* and *panzershrecks*, as well as mines, mortar fire and artillery fire. At the very least, the sandbags reduced the munitions' effects even if they did penetrate the sandbags and organic armor of a vehicle. Adding sandbags to armored vehicles did not significantly reduce the effectiveness of enemy fire from tanks, self-propelled guns and towed anti-tank guns.

As stated by Major Boal, sandbags and, by default, other forms of improvised armor did not fare well when outmatched by enemy high-velocity AP rounds. However, some reported exceptions instilled a degree of confidence in US Army tankers, which made them a morale-booster.

An example of improvised armor providing the crews of M4 tanks a degree of protection appears in a quote by Technical Sergeant Richard T. Heyd of the 2nd Armored Division. The statement appears in the *United States vs. German Equipment* report of March 1945:

> Of a total of nineteen tanks hit, seventeen tanks had been penetrated while only two tanks had withstood the force of the enemy high-velocity shells and ricocheted the projectiles. These ricochets were due to the added protection of sandbags and logs used to reinforce the armor plate in front of the tank.

Improvised Armor in the PTO

From a US Marine Corps report dated May 1945, there is a description of some improvised armor arrangements that appeared during the fighting on the island of Iwo Jima. These included the following: 'Reinforced concrete and lumber placed on tank sponsons and spare track block welded on turrets and front slope plates proved effective counter-measures for both the 47mm fire and shaped charges.'

A very successful arrangement involved a combination of common building materials. These included steel reinforcing rods, heavy 1.5in wire mesh, 2in oak lumber and concrete. According to the report, 'This modification proved invaluable as it enabled the tanks so equipped to withstand shaped-charge explosives and 47mm AP hits on the sponsons. Tanks not equipped in this manner had their sponson armor easily penetrated by 47mm projectiles and shaped charges.'

Flame-Thrower Sherman Tanks in the ETO

In 1943, the US Army's interest in a specially-designed flame-thrower-equipped Sherman tank grew for possible employment during the proposed invasion of France in 1944. Like the British Army flame-thrower tank based on the Churchill and officially nicknamed the 'Crocodile', the Sherman-based version was to have a towed trailer containing the fuel supply.

Unlike the British Army Crocodile, with its flame-thrower gun fitted into the bow machine-gun position, the Sherman version had its flame-thrower gun fitted in a small turret on the right-hand side of the vehicle's front hull. The US Army would eventually order 115 examples for construction by British industry.

The first completed example of the flame-thrower Sherman appeared in March 1944. However, British industry had serious issues in trying to fulfill the demand for the Churchill Crocodile, let alone the US Army's

Sherman version. As a result, only four examples of the Sherman Crocodile were completed, too late to be deployed during Operation OVERLORD. Lack of interest led to cancelation of the program in August 1944. The four were eventually pulled from storage and assigned to a tank battalion of the Ninth Army in November 1944, seeing action only once on February 24, 1945.

With the end of the Sherman Crocodile program in August 1944, the US Army in the ETO's interest turned once again to a tank-mounted auxiliary flame-thrower, most often referred to as the E4-5 Flame Gun. It would replace the .30 caliber bow machine gun on selected Sherman tanks. Those Sherman tanks were so equipped to hopefully play a useful role when encountering the German Westwall defensive fortifications (also known as the Siegfried Line).

Despite uneven performance, the auxiliary flame-throwers mounted on Sherman tanks would continue to see limited use during the remainder of the war in the ETO. In a British Army report titled *The Characteristics and Tactical Employment of Specialised Armour* is this passage on the usefulness of mechanized flame-throwers:

> Field fortifications such as concrete pillboxes can be neutralized or made untenable by flame. The normal reaction of the enemy in such fortifications is to close the gun embrasures, thus becoming blind and unable to fire their weapons. Fuel projected through weapon slits by ricochet may splash on the defenders and will fill the inside with smoke and fumes, which will have an asphyxiating effect on the occupants and thus force them to surrender.

Due to some unforeseen problems, only a small number of the auxiliary flame-throwers made it to the front lines in time to see use against German Westwall defensive positions. Results were mixed: some thought they were helpful, others did not. In the after-action report of the 741st Tank Battalion for September 18–19, 1944 is this extract: 'A flame-thrower tank was used on one pillbox, but the flame-thrower had to approach within 20 yards of the pillbox, and even then the flame was very unsatisfactory.' For the tankers on the flame-thrower-equipped Sherman tanks, approaching that close to a German pillbox put them within the effective range of enemy hand-held anti-tank weapons.

Flame-Thrower Sherman Tanks in the PTO

Besides the use of the auxiliary flame-thrower gun E4-5 fitted in place of a Sherman tank's bow machine gun in the PTO, two later-version arrangements appeared that were fitted alongside the assistant driver/bow

The Sherman Tank from the Driver's Seat

Marc Sehring, manager of the Virginia Museum of Military Vehicles, has this to say about driving the Sherman tank:

From the driver's position, the Sherman in all its variants is roomy with a decent seat. One reason it is roomy is due to its high silhouette caused by the need to pass the center-mounted drive-shaft off a radial under the turret basket. This issue was remedied on later tanks but caused them to be more cramped.

The motors are, for the most part, reliable and easy to maintain except for the multi-bank. I prefer the radial and the Ford GAA the most. The radial is reliable and has a great sound even though it is a bit underpowered compared to the GAA. The GAA has sufficient horsepower and a very deep sound.

From a restoration and repair standpoint, the Sherman series is reasonably simple, and trouble-shooting is straightforward. The twin 6/71 General Motors diesels were good, but diesel fuel was difficult to get and was better for Marine units where Navy diesel was abundant. Then there was the Chrysler multi-bank. This was an engineering disaster, five six-cylinder motors mated together. The multi-bank, thankfully, was used only in training by the Americans but was given to some of our allies.

As a driver, the Sherman is not an easy tank to master. You are dealing with a 65,000lb-plus vehicle with a manual transmission. The clutch is stiff, the transmission takes a strong arm, and steering can be difficult. The suspension used the volute springs and made for a much rougher ride than later torsion bar suspension tanks.

Steering the Sherman takes strong arms and back. Depending on ground conditions and the type of track you are using, steering can be very tiring. During this period, American tanks used a type of differential steering, which made for a poor turning radius. The Russians, Germans and British all designed vehicles with improved turning radius over the Americans but proved less reliable.

I still find the Sherman fun to drive, but it does make you work for it. It makes you appreciate what our soldiers had to fight in.

gunner's hatch-mounted overhead periscope. These arrangements had limited usefulness due to their short range and inadequate fuel capacity.

The preferred Sherman tank-based flame-thrower configuration in the PTO involved the replacement of the tank's 75mm main gun with the POA-CWS-H1 flame gun and the addition of larger fuel tanks. The first eight examples, based on M4A3 Medium Tanks, landed on Iwo Jima on February 19, 1945. They proved very useful, as well as popular with their crews.

In the meantime, the Army armed fifty-four M4 Medium Tanks (composite hull version) with the POA-CWS-H1 flame guns. They would arrive in Okinawa on April 7, 1945. In a May 1949 research report prepared for the Armored School, titled *Armor on Okinawa,* is an extract from the After-Action Report by the 763rd Tank Battalion on the use of the flame-thrower tanks during the battle:

> It is difficult to over-emphasize the importance of the role played by these [flame-thrower] tanks. Working closely with standard tanks and infantry, they were invaluable in clearing out the strong enemy positions ... The demand for flame-throwers [tanks] always exceeded the supply. Action during this period was characterized by huge numbers of Japs being destroyed by tanks, after being flushed out of caves by flame-throwers.

Pictured here is the Medium Tank T6, the first iteration of the M4 series of medium tanks. To speed up its development, as many components of the M3 Medium Tank series as possible were incorporated into its design. These included the upper hull side armored doors, the vehicle commander's machine-gun-armed cupola, the air-cooled, gasoline-powered radial engine and the early vertical volute suspension spring (VVSS) system. *(National Archives)*

An early-production M4A1 Medium Tank. By this point, the upper hull side armored doors of the Medium Tank T6 and the vehicle commander's machine-gun-armed cupola had disappeared. The latter was replaced by a two-piece split hatch. The M4A1 had a single armored port on the left-hand side of the turret for dispensing with spent cartridge cases. (*TACOM*)

The vertical sides of the welded-hull M4 Medium Tank proved roomier than the rounded upper hull of the M4A1 Medium Tank. This allowed for more authorized main gun ammunition storage. Whereas the M4A1 had room for ninety main gun rounds, the M4 had space for ninety-seven main gun rounds. The amount of authorized small-arms ammunition was the same on both tanks. (*Patton Museum*)

(**Opposite, above**) The T6 Medium Tank featured, besides a bow .30 caliber machine gun in a flexible mount, two fixed forward-firing .30 caliber machine guns. That same design feature appeared on very early-production M4 series tanks such as the museum-piece M4A1 pictured here, with one gun slightly elevated. (*Pierre-Olivier Buan*)

(**Opposite, below**) Early-production M4 series medium tanks had six suspension assembly units, three on either side of the hull. The track return roller was located at the top. On later-production M4 series medium tanks, the return roller was attached to a trailing arm bracket located behind each suspension assembly unit as is visible in this photograph. (*Patton Museum*)

(**Above**) Pictured here is the turret of the second production M4A1 Medium Tank. Like the T6 Medium Tank, it came with a 'sight rotor' for the gunner. It is pictured with its pivoting armored flap in the closed position. The US Army disliked the device and no more than forty tanks were built with the feature. Pictorial evidence shows that at least one example made it to Italy with the US Army. (*Pierre-Olivier Buan*)

(**Above**) The sight rotor's replacement was the fixed overhead periscope pictured here, which included a sighting reticle for the gunner, a design feature seen on all subsequent M4 series tanks. Next to the gunner's periscope sight is the first version of a metal vane sight, which allowed the vehicle commander, with his head above his cupola, to roughly line up the main gun with a potential target by verbally directing the gunner to its location. (*Pierre-Olivier Buan*)

(**Opposite, above**) The tank pictured here has the original gun shield, which was labeled the M34 Combination Gun Mount. The narrow curved armored piece over the gun shield is referred to as a 'rotor shield'. Its purpose was to prevent bullet splash from jamming the 75mm main gun in elevation. The gun shield was 3in thick and the rotor shield 2in thick. (*Pierre-Olivier Buan*)

(**Opposite, below**) The M4 series driver had the form-fitted seat with a padded back-rest, pictured here, as did the bow gunner/assistant driver. Each seat fitted onto a pedestal that was adjustable for height. Visible are the two vertical steering brake levers and gearshift lever to the right of the driver's seat. Also seen to the right of the driver's seat is the tank's transmission. (*Pierre-Olivier Buan*)

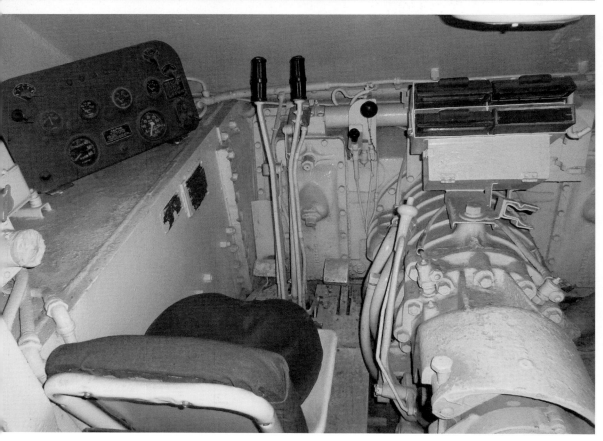

(**Above**) A rear view of the powertrain assembly for an M4 series medium tank. Projecting from the left-hand side is one of its two drive sprockets, minus the track-driving sprocket fixture. The powertrain assembly incorporated the tank's differential, steering brakes and final drives in the same removable armored housing. Bolted directly to the rear of the powertrain assembly is the vehicle's transmission. (*Pierre-Olivier Buan*)

(**Opposite, above**) The CHA final drive housing (covering the powertrain assembly) of M4 series medium tanks came in two basic styles. The original seen here consisted of three pieces that bolted together. It derived from that developed for the M3 series of medium tanks. User feedback indicated that it lacked rigidity and was more readily penetrated by anti-tank gun projectiles. (*Pierre-Olivier Buan*)

(**Opposite, below**) To increase reliability and protection, the new and improved one-piece final drive housing pictured here entered into production in April 1942. Variations of the three-piece and one-piece CHA final drive housings reflected the large number of foundries involved in their construction. (*Richard and Barb Eshleman*)

The Medium Tank T6 and early-production M4 series medium tanks provided their drivers and bow gunners with two methods of observation when their overhead hatches were closed. First, a rotating periscope was incorporated into each overhead hatch. Second, in front of each crewman was a direct vision slot protected by an armored flap as pictured here. Each flap could be opened or closed from within the tank. (*Pierre-Olivier Buan*)

As the direct vision ports on early-production M4 series medium tanks allowed bullet splash to enter the crew compartment, they were discontinued. In their place, the factories eventually added what is referred to in contemporary terms as 'hatch hoods', as seen in this picture. They incorporated a fixed periscope in front of the driver's and bow gunner's overhead hatches. Each overhead hatch incorporated a rotating periscope which provided improved lateral vision. (*Pierre-Olivier Buan*)

Taking part in a military vehicle demonstration is an M3A1 Light Tank. The initial version of the M3 light tank series supplied to the British Army in North Africa proved to be the M3 Light Tank. Externally, the prominent spotting feature between the two light tanks, the vehicle commander's cupola on the M3 Light Tank, was discontinued on the follow-up M3A1 Light Tank. (*Ian Wilcox*)

In US Army markings, an M3A1 Light Tank. Unlike the original M3 Light Tank, which lacked a rotating turret basket, the M3A1 – thanks in part to British Army experience – had a turret basket fitted to improve crew efficiency. On the M3 Light Tank, the two-man turret crew had to step over the enclosed drive train located at the bottom of the tank's hull. (*Dreamtime*)

Intended for use by US Army airborne divisions was the Light Tank M22 pictured here. The original plans called for the vehicle's turret to be removed and carried inside the fuselage of a four-engine cargo plane. The vehicle's hull was to be attached to the bottom of the aircraft's fuselage. Upon flying into a captured enemy airport, the tank was to be reassembled. The tank never saw use with the US Army during the Second World War. (*Pierre-Olivier Buan*)

The US Army's replacement for the M3 and M5 series of light tanks proved to be the M24 Light Tank pictured here. It was armed with a 75mm gun initially designed for mounting in the nose of B-25 medium bombers. The vehicle received power from the same two V-8 Cadillac car engines that went into the M5 Light Tank series. (*Pierre-Olivier Buan*)

The British Army version of the American-designed and built M3 Medium Tank series is seen here, which the British designated 'the Grant'. The prominent external spotting feature is its much larger CHA turret. The British Army wanted the vehicle's radio in the rear of the turret for easy access by the vehicle commander. (*Pierre-Olivier Buan*)

The chassis of the British Army Grant tanks included almost every version of the M3 series of medium tanks built. The example pictured here is the original M3 Medium Tank. American factories would build Grant-configured tanks from August 1941 until July 1942. They first saw action with the British Army in the spring of 1942 in the Battle of Gazala.

(*Pierre-Olivier Buan*)

The mainstay of the US Army in the Second World War: the M4 series of medium tanks, both first- and second-generation. Pictured here is a first-generation M4A1 with its CHA hull/turret armed with a 75mm main gun. American factories built 6,281 examples of this model between February 1942 and December 1943. (*Ian Wilcox*)

Beside the CHA hull first-generation M4A1 Medium Tank, the largest number of M4 series medium tanks built was the welded RHA hull versions, with an example of an M4A3 pictured here, armed with a 75mm gun. Between June and September 1943, 1,690 examples of the first-generation M4A3 came off the assembly lines. (*Pierre-Olivier Buan*)

As the gasoline-powered and liquid-cooled Ford GAA engine proved to be the most reliable and robust of the gasoline engines installed in first-generation M4 series medium tanks, the M4A3 Medium Tank became the US Army's preferred model. Pictured here is a second-generation M4A3 Medium Tank, with its reset glacis and larger front hull hatches. (*Chun-lun Hsu*)

Shown here is a second-generation M4A1 Medium Tank armed with a 76mm main gun. In that configuration it became the M4A1 (76) W, as recorded on its data plate. The 76mm gun came about by direction of the Ordnance Department, which remained concerned that first-generation M4s' 75mm guns' AP rounds were decreasingly able to penetrate German tank armor, leaving the US tanks at a serious disadvantage. (*Pierre-Olivier Buan*)

The M4A3 (76) W, the preferred second-generation version of the M4 series of medium tanks armed with a 76mm main gun, is pictured here. Unlike early-production 76mm gun-armed M4 series medium tanks, the example seen here is riding on the improved Horizontal Volute Spring Suspension (HVSS) system. (*Pierre-Olivier Buan*)

A variant of the M4 series of medium tanks, the second-generation M4A3 seen here armed with a 105mm howitzer. The example pictured is riding on an HVSS system. Despite the second-generation reset glacis and the larger hatches, the M4A3 (105) did not include wet stowage due to the size of the main gun rounds. (*WW2 Armor Museum*)

The senior leadership of the US Army believed early on that the German Army had pre-vailed over the French Army due to masses of tanks in the summer of 1940. The US Army came up with the concept of dedicated tank destroyers, such as the M10 pictured here, as the answer. (*Pierre-Olivier Buan*)

Supplied with 1,648 examples of the M10 Tank Destroyer under Lend-Lease, the British Army concluded that the M10's 3in (76.2mm) gun lacked the penetrative power to deal with thickly-armored German tanks. In its place, they mounted their much more power-ful 17-pounder (76.2mm) gun, as seen here. (*Pierre-Olivier Buan*)

Pictured here is another American-designed-and-built tank destroyer, the M18 GMC. A lightweight vehicle riding on a torsion bar suspension system, it was powered by a radial engine coupled to a new state-of-the-art automatic transmission. The M18 could reach maximum speed on level roads of 60mph, making it the fastest armored fighting vehicle of the Second World War. (*WW2 Armor Museum*)

The US Army's eventual answer to late-war German tanks was the M26 Pershing Heavy Tank pictured here. Armed with the same 90mm main gun as the M36 Tank Destroyer, it had the thick armor protection the M36 lacked. The enclosed turret, as well its bow and coaxial machine guns, gave it the means to deal with enemy infantry at close ranges. (*Pierre-Olivier Buan*)

It did not take long before the new protruding hatch hoods' vertical face, especially on welded-hull M4 and M4A3 Medium Tanks, were understood to be ballistic weak spots more readily penetrated by enemy fire. Due to cast-hull M4A1 Medium Tanks' more rounded shape of their hatch, hoods were not as much of a risk. To correct the problem, slightly angled 1.5in RHA plates were welded in place on both welded and CHA upper hulls, as seen here. (*Pierre-Olivier Buan*)

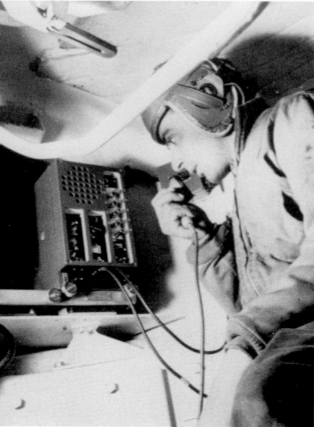

From the gunner's position on an M4 series medium tank looking rearward at the turret bustle is the loader operating the vehicle's FM radio. The metal bar seen in the picture is a portion of the 75mm main gun's recoil guard. Some tank crews removed it to make it easier for the loader to leave the turret in a hurry if his position in the vehicle in question lacked an overhead hatch. (*Patton Museum*)

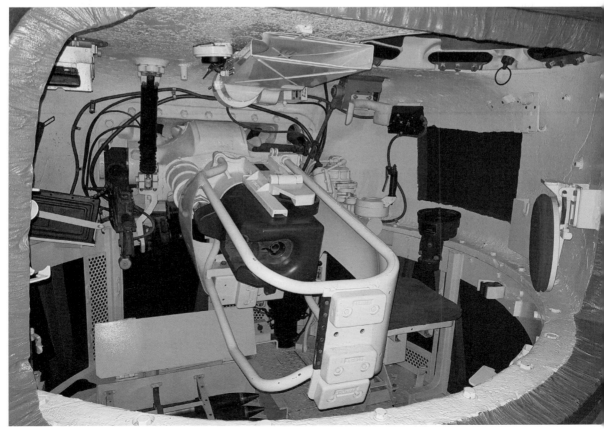

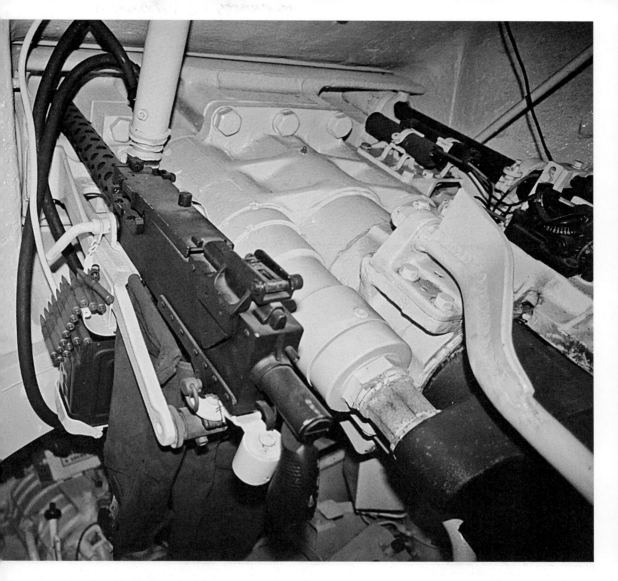

(**Opposite, above**) From an M4 series wartime manual is this illustration of the recessed ball-bearing turret race assembly (also referred to unofficially as the turret ring) on which a tank's turret rotated. Below the ring is the turret basket, which bolted to the turret ring and rotated with the turret in either manual or power traverse modes. (*Patton Museum*)

(**Opposite, below**) Looking into an M4 series medium tank turret trainer from its rear, one can see the breech end of the 75mm Gun M3 and the recoil guard surrounding it for crew protection. The loader's (also referred to as the cannoneer in wartime manuals) position is on the left of the gun. The gunner sat on the right of the gun, and the commander sat behind and above him. (*Hans Halbertstadt*)

(**Above**) Attached on the left-hand side of the M4 series tanks' 75mm gun mount is a .30 caliber machine gun labeled the 'coaxial'. It was the tank's most useful weapon and fired most often. The authorized storage for .30 caliber rounds onboard was 4,750. Both the gunner and loader could fire the coaxial. (*Hans Halbertstadt*)

(**Above**) Seen on the floor of an M4 series medium tank's turret basket is an armored container for eight 75mm main gun rounds, referred to as the 'ready rack'. Rather than the first rounds loaded and fired, they were to be the last. In theory, according to wartime manuals, all the other main gun rounds in the tank were to be fired first before resorting to the ready rack rounds. (*Hans Halbertstadt*)

(**Opposite, above left**) The 75mm Gun M3 fired a number of different rounds, some examples of which are pictured here. On the left, Armor-Piercing M72 Shot-Tracer (AP-T); in the middle, High-Explosive (HE) M48 Shell, which came in two different versions, listed as Supercharge or Normal. The right-hand round bore the designation HC B1 M89 Shell, Smoke, and would typically be referred to as White Phosphorus (WP), unofficially nicknamed 'Willy-Pete'. (*World War Two Armor Museum*)

(**Opposite, above right**) The majority of 75mm main gun rounds were divided between three horizontal sponson racks in the M4 series. These were originally unprotected, but later enclosed in armor containers as pictured here. This was done to better protect the vehicle's crew. (*Author's collection*)

(**Opposite, below**) US Army tankers in the ETO are seen loading their tank with main gun rounds, always a laborious and time-consuming process. An armor-penetrating round for the 75mm gun on the M4 series tank was the M61 Armor-Piercing Capped-Tracer (APC-T). The complete round weighed about 20lb. (*Patton Museum*)

(**Above**) Instead of the T6 Medium Tank's CHA machine-gun-armed cupola, originally all early-production M4 series tanks had the same overhead vehicle commander's two-piece split-hatch as seen here. The design came from that fitted on the British Army's Grant tank. As with so many other design features on the M4 series, it went through a number of progressive improvements. (*Pierre-Olivier Buan*)

(**Opposite, above**) Field reports resulted in the addition of an overhead oval hatch for the M4 series tank loader's position, beginning at the factories in November/December 1943. The protruding circular object in front of the vehicle commander's and loader's hatch is the upper portion of the turret ventilator. (*Pierre-Olivier Buan*)

(**Opposite, below**) The replacement for the original vehicle commander's split-hatch is visible in this picture. Referred to as the 'Cupola, Commander's Vision', it was approved for use in December 1943. Around its periphery were six evenly-spaced laminated glass vision blocks. To better protect the gunner's fixed overhead periscope, there appeared a three-sided armored enclosure, topped by a sheet metal cover, as pictured here. Also visible is the second model sight vane. (*Pierre-Olivier Buan*)

(**Above**) British and American tankers disliked the gunner's periscope sight on the M4 series, believing it inaccurate. They wanted a direct-sight telescope. The long exterior openings for the new direct-sight telescope and the coaxial machine gun were considered ballistic weak spots with the M34 Combination Gun Mount (gun shield). The M34's replacement, the M34A1 Combination Gun Mount (gun shield) pictured here, included a full-width rotor shield. (*Pierre-Olivier Buan*)

(**Opposite, above**) The front upper hull (especially the glacis) on welded-hull M4 Medium Tanks proved time-consuming to construct due to the large number of welds needed to accommodate the protruding hatch hoods. The many weld seams also reduced the ballistic strength of the tank's glacis. The solution: weld onto the front upper hull of an M4 Medium Tank the CHA front upper hull of an M4A1 Medium Tank, as pictured here. (*Patton Museum*)

(**Opposite, below**) Lessons learned from the fighting in North Africa: the vulnerability of the upper hull (sponson) storage for 75mm main gun rounds to enemy fire. This resulted in the addition of three armored patches to those locations where rounds were stored. Shown here are the two armored (appliqué) patches to the right-hand side of the upper hull of a diesel-engine-powered M4A2 Medium Tank. (*Patton Museum*)

Here a gunner on a 75mm-gun-armed M4 series tank is looking through his periscope sight. Later-production tanks added a direct-sight telescope to supplement the periscope sight. Typically, it was the vehicle commander who identified targets. He then informed the gunner in which direction they lay. The gunner then used his power traverse system to lay the gun on the target, with the aid of verbal input from the vehicle commander.
(*Patton Museum*)

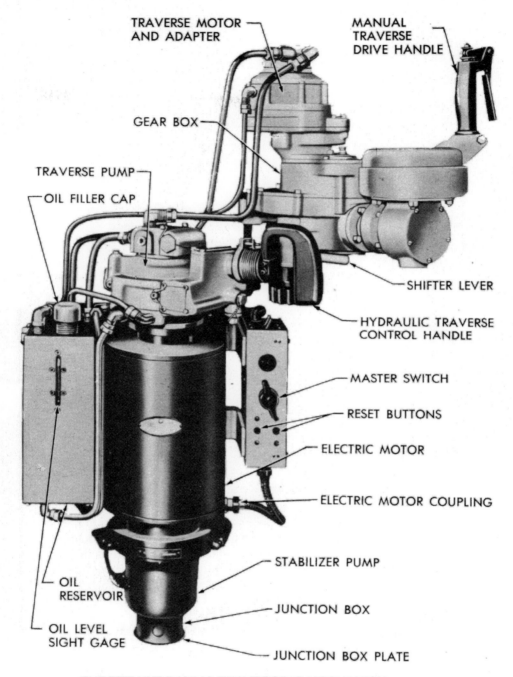

TRAVERSE MOTOR AND ADAPTER

MANUAL TRAVERSE DRIVE HANDLE

GEAR BOX

TRAVERSE PUMP

OIL FILLER CAP

SHIFTER LEVER

HYDRAULIC TRAVERSE CONTROL HANDLE

MASTER SWITCH

RESET BUTTONS

ELECTRIC MOTOR

ELECTRIC MOTOR COUPLING

STABILIZER PUMP

OIL RESERVOIR

JUNCTION BOX

OIL LEVEL SIGHT GAGE

JUNCTION BOX PLATE

TURRET HYDRAULIC TRAVERSING MECHANISM

From a wartime manual is this image of the electro-hydraulic power traverse system. It proved to be the more common of two different systems fitted to M4 series tanks. A gunner needed only 17 seconds to rotate the tank's turret 360 degrees with the power traverse system. A shortage of electro-hydraulic power traverse systems led to some M4 series tanks having an all-electric power traverse system fitted instead. (*Patton Museum*)

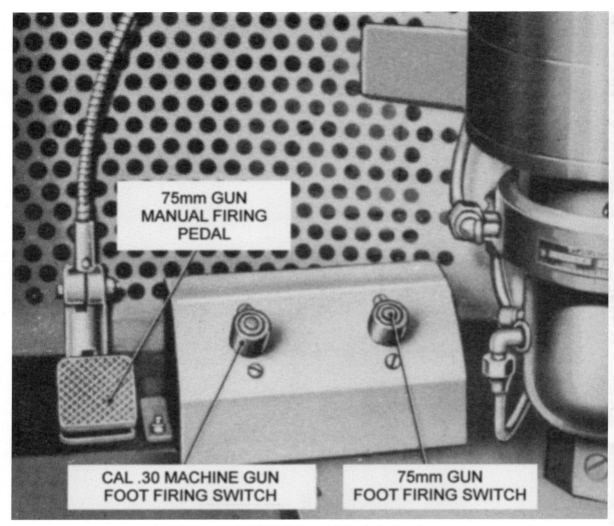

75mm GUN MANUAL FIRING PEDAL

CAL .30 MACHINE GUN FOOT FIRING SWITCH

75mm GUN FOOT FIRING SWITCH

(**Above**) Located on the turret basket floor on M4 series tanks are the gunner's foot-operated electrical firing switches. Upon the loader inserting a round into the main gun, he would either verbally inform the gunner that a round was ready or kick him in the left shin with his right foot, documented in wartime manuals. It normally fell to the vehicle commander to actually give the gunner the order to fire. (*Patton Museum*)

(**Opposite, above**) During production of early-model M4 series tanks, it became necessary to thin the interior of the turret wall, just in front of the gunner's position, to provide enough room for the turret's power traverse system. Unfortunately, this resulted in a weak spot in the tank's ballistic protection. To resolve the issue, an armored (appliqué) patch, as seen here, covered the location. (*Pierre-Olivier Buan*)

(**Opposite, below**) With America's official entry into the Second World War and a great increase in tank as well as aircraft construction, the demand for radial engines exceeded supply. The US Army had to consider alternatives. The most promising was a modification of a liquid-cooled, gasoline-powered, experimental eight-cylinder aircraft engine seen here that was developed by the Ford Motor Company and labeled the Ford GAA. (*Public domain*)

(**Opposite, above**) As a tank engine, the Ford GAA went into a welded-hull M4 series tank, which so fitted became the M4A3 Medium Tank pictured here. All welded-hull M4 series tanks looked the same from a distance. As one got closer, one saw their different design features, especially the rear engine compartment arrangements. A readily visible rear hull feature that identifies the M4A3 Medium Tank is the exhaust deflector visible in this picture. (*Pierre-Olivier Buan*)

(**Opposite, below**) Looking at the lower rear engine compartment of an M4A1 Medium Tank, plainly visible are the two large engine access doors. On either side, under the cut-out rear upper hull section, are the circular engine air cleaners. The engine exhaust air cleaners also came in a square variation. The two engine exhaust vents are just under the rear upper hull overhang. (*Pierre-Olivier Buan*)

(**Above**) Despite introduction of the Ford GAA engine, as well as the Model 6046 twin-engine diesel powerplant arrangement in the M4A2 Medium Tank, there remained a shortage of engines for all the M4 series tanks built. The US Army therefore approved installing the Chrysler A57 Multibank powerplant seen here for installation in the M4 series. The resulting tank became the M4A4 Medium Tank. (*Public domain*)

(**Above**) The turret of an M4A1 Medium Tank that has been blown off its tank, either by the crew using a demolition charge or penetration by an enemy projectile that resulted in detonation of the main gun rounds. Also visible in the image is the open pistol port on the left-hand side of the turret. The name pistol port is a misnomer, as tank crews used it as a main gun reloading hatch and to dispense with spent cartridge cases. (*National Archives*)

(**Opposite, above**) An M4A1 is seen here with a large-caliber projectile having penetrated to one side of the bow gunner/assistant driver's hatch hood. British Army efforts in France in determining what type of gun had fired such shots proved futile, as tank crews could not reliably identify which weapon had engaged them. (*Patton Museum*)

(**Opposite, below**) An American soldier appears to be looking at damage caused to an M4 Medium Tank that had taken a large high-velocity armor-piercing round, penetrating the vehicle's CHA final drive housing. The blackened turret and 75mm gun barrel indicate that the tank's main gun ammunition had caught fire. (*National Archives*)

As the poor level of protection offered by the armor on the M4 series became clear to US Army tankers in the European Theater of Operation (ETO), there began to appear a wide array of improvised armor arrangements, as seen here. Other tankers covered their vehicles with sandbags and even cement. (*National Archives*)

The M4 series tanks in the PTO faced far less of a threat from the enemy's inventory of anti-tank guns. The most numerous Japanese towed anti-tank gun, a 37mm weapon, was eventually supplemented by the larger 47mm towed anti-tank gun pictured here, which could penetrate the glacis of M4 series tanks. (*Chris Hughes*)

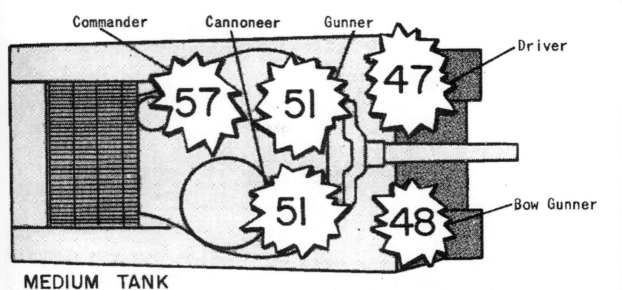

Commander — 57
Cannoneer — 51
Gunner — 47
Driver
51
48
Bow Gunner

MEDIUM TANK

From a wartime report, an illustration of the percentage of casualties by crew position on M4 series tanks. It's no surprise that vehicle commanders suffered the highest loss rate, as they tended to have their heads exposed over the lip of their overhead hatch or vision cupola for the best visibility.

Pictured here are Marine Corps M4A2 Medium Tanks on Iwo Jima in February 1945. Note the steel tracks on the tanks shown. These originally came about due to a rubber shortage that began in December 1941. By June 1942, it was anticipated that all M4 series medium tank tracks were to be steel. However, a continued demand for rubber tracks kept them in production throughout the Second World War. (*National Archives*)

(**Opposite, above**) During a training demonstration, a front hull-mounted M3-4-3 flame-thrower gun is seen in action. The weapon took the place of the .30 caliber bow machine gun. It had an effective range of approximately 60 yards, with the flame gun raised at an elevation of 10 degrees. (*Patton Museum*)

(**Opposite, below**) Visible in this photograph is the M3-4-3 auxiliary flame-thrower gun fitted in place of the .30 caliber bow machine gun in an M4 Medium Tank. Another design had the flame-thrower gun nozzle projected out of the bow gunner/assistant driver's overhead hatch. (*National Archives*)

(**Above**) The popularity of flame-thrower tanks in the Pacific would not be apparent in Europe. This was due to the late-1944 delivery of the auxiliary flame-thrower guns, as well as a general lack of enthusiasm by the user community in the theater. Pictured here is one of only four modified M4 series tanks, unofficially nicknamed 'the Sherman Crocodile', which had a flame-thrower gun mounted in a small front upper hull-mounted turret as is visible here. (*National Archives*)

When the US Army's armored divisions were shipped overseas, they received new production tanks. A program began in December 1943 and continued until May 1945 to reclaim and rebuild the divisions' original tanks with as many new product features as possible at the lowest cost. Pictured here is an example of an early-production M4A1 fitted with extended end connectors and the late-model vehicle commander cupola. (*Patton Museum*)

Chapter Four

Late War M4 Tanks

The Ordnance Department began considering an improved version of the Sherman tank in February 1942, the same month that the first M4A1 Medium Tank rolled off the factory floor. Their design study envisioned a tank with a thicker and better-sloped welded RHA upper hull. Thicker armor entailed increased weight, which in turn mandated a more powerful engine and drivetrain, as well as a sturdier suspension system.

Armament for an improved Sherman tank would remain the standard M3 75mm Gun that had first appeared on the M3 Medium Tank series. Instead of a CHA turret, a welded RHA turret appeared able to mount either a 3in (76.2mm) gun or a 105mm howitzer.

The negative design features of the proposed improved Sherman that led to it never progressing past the concept stage were twofold. First, the tank's main gun rounds were to remain stowed in the upper hull sponsons, already considered a very undesirable location. Second, the vehicle's fuel tanks were to be relocated from the engine compartment to a new location at the bottom of the lower hull, just below the turret basket, another very vulnerable position and undesirable for morale and crew survivability.

The Next Step

With the proposed improved Sherman concept falling by the wayside, the Ordnance Department began considering a stopgap policy of up-gunning the existing first-generation M4A1 Sherman tank to deal with the German up-armed and up-armored Mark IV Medium Tank series.

At first, the idea of the 76.2mm gun from the M6 Heavy Tank (which never entered front-line service) received consideration. In place of the 76.2mm gun from the M6 Heavy Tank, a crash development program began for a lighter version.

The new lightweight weapon fired the same projectile as the original gun but with a smaller cartridge case. To provide it with the same muzzle velocity as the 76.2mm gun with the smaller cartridge case, it used a more powerful propellant charge.

To prevent confusion between the two same-caliber tank guns firing two different-sized main gun rounds, the 76.2mm gun on the M6 Heavy

Tank became the 3in Gun M7. The new version mounted in the turret of the pilot M4A1 received the test designation of T1.

Testing of a pilot M4A1 armed with the new 76.2mm Gun T1 showed that the gun unbalanced the turret, making the turret difficult to traverse when the tank was on steep slopes. The initial solution involved removing 15in from the muzzle end of the gun; the shorter-barreled 76.2mm gun received the designation M1. Shortening the barrel unfortunately reduced the muzzle velocity of the gun's standard AP round, which in turn reduced its armor penetration ability, making the weapon less effective.

Instead of listing the M1 as a 76.2mm gun, the Army referred to it as a 76mm gun. Like follow-on models, the M1 fired an HE round and two different types of AP rounds. These included the M62 APC-T, with a muzzle velocity of 2,600 ft per second and an AP-T shot round with the same muzzle velocity. The M62 APC-T weighed 24.8lb, compared to the M61 APC-T round for the 75mm Gun M3 which weighed 19.2lb.

Some Issues

Despite shortening the 76mm Gun M1, its weight remained an issue. The solution was to add extra weight to the gun's recoil guard and turret bustle. Despite the up-gunned M4A1 prototype's design shortcomings, the prototype proved acceptable as a stopgap design. The Ordnance Department proposed an order for 1,000 examples in August 1942, designated the M4A1 (76M1).

Despite the Ordnance Department's acceptance, Lieutenant General Jacob Devers, commander of the Armored Force, disapproved. He complained that the Armored Board of the Armored Force had not yet had a chance to test the vehicle properly.

To placate Devers, in August 1942 Ordnance ordered twelve additional examples of the improvised up-gunned tank for testing. The tanks arrived in February 1943 and the test reports concluded that the vehicles' turret had insufficient space for the crew to perform their roles properly, making it unfit for use in the field. That decision effectively ended the program.

A British Gun

During a December 1942 visit to North Africa and then England, Devers and other high-ranking US Army officers witnessed firepower demonstrations of both towed and tank-mounted configurations of the British Army's new 17-pounder (76.2mm) gun. The British gun's performance greatly impressed Devers, inspiring him to push for the 76mm gun on a Sherman tank.

The 17-pounder's initial prototype in a towed configuration appeared in the spring of 1942. Besides an HE round, it fired an APC-T (shot) round at 2,900 ft per second. It first saw combat as a towed anti-tank gun with the British Army in North Africa in February 1943.

For the tank-mounted version of the 17-pounder, there appeared what the British Army labeled a Super-Velocity Discarding Sabot (SVDS) shot round in August 1944. It had a muzzle velocity of 3,950 ft per second. More speed meant improved penetration at short and medium ranges. In the US Army, the same type of round bore the label of Armor-Piercing Discarding Sabot (APDS).

The British had offered the 17-pounder gun design to the US Army in August 1943, but the offer was declined for several reasons. One was the US Army's confidence that its upcoming 76mm and 90mm guns were more than adequate to handle heavily-armored German tanks. In contrast, the British Army had by that time of the war acquired a much better appreciation of German tanks' constant armor upgrades and what it might take to destroy them in battle.

Back to the Drawing Board

By early 1943 the Ordnance Department had concluded that there would be no time to develop and field a new medium tank to replace the first-generation Sherman tanks. Therefore, it decided the only recourse would be an upgraded second-generation Sherman tank series.

The initial effort to develop a second-generation Sherman tank had begun on the same day that the Ordnance Committee had put an end to the M4A1 (76M1). On June 17, 1943 they had given the go-ahead for two pilot examples of a Sherman tank designated the M4E6, armed with a modified version of the 76mm Gun M1 designated the M1A1. Both M4E6 pilots, delivered in July 1943, had a composite upper hull configuration.

To answer the Armored Forces' biggest complaint about the M4A1 (76M1) – i.e. the cramped turret – a new larger CHA turret went onto the M4A6, similar to that produced for the never-fielded T23 Medium Tank. The larger turret also came with a new full-width gun shield for the 76mm Gun M1A1. Also, under consideration but not implemented for the M4E6, was a welded RHA turret initially contemplated for the T23 Medium Tank.

A Novel Solution

Another design modification for the M4E6 involved moving the main gun ammunition storage racks from the sponsons to a location under the turret basket. The 76mm rounds would reside in containers filled with a water/anti-freeze/anti-rust mixture to lessen the threat of ammunition fires. The theory was that if penetrated by metal fragments, these containers would release their liquid contents and extinguish main gun ammunition fires, although some who worked on the project harbored doubts about its effectiveness.

The new main gun ammunition storage arrangement in the M4E6 received the label 'wet stowage', eventually shortened to just 'Wet' on second-generation tank data plates. First-generation Sherman tanks without that design feature were subsequently referred to as 'dry stowage' tanks in War Department manuals.

Combat experience in the ETO would eventually demonstrate that Sherman tanks with wet stowage suffered fewer catastrophic kills than their first-generation counterparts. The consensus was that relocation of the main gun rounds to the bottom of the tank hulls had more to do with their survival than the liquid-filled containers.

Some Points to be Resolved

Testing of the two M4E6 tanks went well, and on August 17, 1943 the Armored Board recommended that the up-armed Sherman be standardized. The AGF concurred and requested 1,000 examples. With manufacture of the M4E6, the AGF wanted to end production of the 75mm gun-armed Sherman tanks.

The Armored Board stated that it wanted to continue production of 75mm gun-armed Sherman tanks as its HE round remained superior to that employed with the 76mm Gun M1A1. The larger gun's only significant advantage was that it could penetrate one more inch of armor plate than the 75mm gun.

The Ordnance Department would claim that the 76mm Gun M1A1 could penetrate the frontal armor of the Tiger I at a range of 2,000 yards. The combat reality was that the German tank's frontal armor was utterly impenetrable by the 76mm Gun M1A1's AP round at any other than extremely close ranges.

90mm Main Gun-Armed Sherman

Even before the Ordnance Department began considering up-arming the Sherman tank with a 76mm main gun, it had been thinking about a Sherman tank armed with a 90mm main gun based on a recently introduced anti-aircraft gun.

An August 31, 1942 report by the Ballistic Research Laboratory, a part of the Ordnance Department, stated that such an arrangement was possible. The interest in a 90mm gun-armed Sherman tank came from combat reports about the successful German employment of their 88mm anti-aircraft gun in the anti-tank role.

The British Army also proved very interested in the idea of a 90mm gun-armed Sherman tank up until the fall of 1943. On October 17, 1943 John F. Evetts, a high-ranking British Army officer, informed US Army Major General Gladeon M. Barnes of the Ordnance Department that a tank-mounted 90mm gun was a must for future operations on the European mainland.

As an experiment, the 90mm Gun M3 fitted in the pre-production turret (of what eventually became the M26 Heavy tank) was tested on an M4 Medium Tank with some second-generation features. In the fall of 1943, the Armored Board requested that 1,000 examples of a 90mm main gun-armed tank be procured based on the M4A3 Medium Tank chassis.

For several reasons, the plan never went anywhere. First, the Ordnance Department began thinking it would be better to mount a 90mm main gun and turret on what later became the M26 Heavy Tank chassis. It also had concerns that the 90mm turret was too heavy for the M4A3 tank chassis.

The Army Ground Forces' (AGFs') senior leadership also remained heavily invested in the doctrine that tanks don't fight tanks, as that was the job of tank destroyers. The AGF also brought up the fact that no theater of operation had indicated a desire for a 90mm gun-armed tank. For example, General Eisenhower, when asked by the War Department in May 1944 whether 90mm gun-armed tank destroyers would prove useful for the invasion of the Continent, replied in the negative.

A passage from the US Army's green multi-volume book series on the Second World War titled *The Ordnance Department on Beachhead and Battle-front* is a reflection on what could have been if the 90mm gun-armed Sherman had received the go-ahead:

> ... modification of a thousand M4s might have been attempted when it was first proposed by the Armored Force Board in September 1943. In retrospect, it seems to have been worth trying, and if successful, it would in some measure have provided tankers with the firepower they needed in Europe, from the break-out [Operation COBRA] to the last defense of the Rhine.

However, other factors offer play into these decisions other than wanting a larger gun. Reliability, AVAILABILITY – no mount yet existed – and then

---

What the Tankers Wanted

From the April 27, 1944 Report of the New Weapon Board is a passage on what American tankers in Italy wanted to see in their tanks:

> Combat troops have definite ideas as to what improvements should be incorporated in tank design. First, the Board inquired as to what they considered the most important features in a tank. The replies were unanimous: the gun was of first consideration; second came dependability; third, whatever armor they could get after the first two requirements were met ... With respect to the gun for the medium tank, they demand larger caliber and higher velocity.

there was the question of balance, and impact of the weight on the turret traversing mechanism, and size of the round in the turret, and weight increase on the suspension, and…higher weight means reduced range on the same fuel tanks, etc.

The Ultimate Design Sherman

In July 1943, as the M4E6 progressed, the Ordnance Department decided to pull together all the various upgrade programs under way for what would become the 76mm gun-armed second generation of Sherman tanks. The official label became the 'Medium Tank M4 Series (Ultimate Design)'.

Design drawings for the up-gunned second-generation M4, M4A1, M4A2 and M4A3 (based on the design work for the M4E6) appeared in December 1943, with pilots intended for testing available starting in February 1944. As events unfolded, the M4 Medium Tank would never receive the second-generation upgrades.

Not waiting for testing of pilot tanks, the first 100 production examples of the second-generation M4A1 came off the factory floor in January 1944 with the data plate designation 'Tank Medium M4A1 76mm Gun, Wet' with deliveries that same month. By July 1945, a total of 3,426 had rolled off the assembly line. (Hereafter, for the sake of brevity, 'Tank Medium M4A1 76mm Gun, Wet' will be identified by the label M4A1 (76) W.)

Late-war US Army tankers verbally referred to their Sherman tanks by the main guns fitted. Hence they were either labeled '75s' or '76s'.

The British Army received 1,330 of the M4A1 (76) W tanks under Lend-Lease, which they labeled the 'Sherman IIA'. As they thought little of the armor penetration capabilities of the 76mm gun, they were initially at a loss what to do with them. In the end most were sent to its armored units in the MTO, as the threat from enemy armor in that theater proved less serious.

In the ETO, the British Army transferred 180 examples of the Sherman IIA to the Free Polish forces to make up for combat losses. The Free French Army in the ETO acquired M4A1 (76) W tanks, not from Lend-Lease but from US Army stockpiles in that theater.

New Front Hull Hatches

The Army's Medical Research Laboratory concluded in February 1943 that the narrow front hull overhead hatches on first-generation Sherman tanks were causing a great many non-combat injuries among crewmen, just in the process of entering and leaving their vehicles. Worse, in combat situations, when every second counted, they made quick entry or especially exit from the vehicle extremely difficult.

Larger overhead front hull hatches seemed to make the most sense. However, it proved impossible to implement due to the existing 57-degree glacis on first-generation Sherman tanks. Work therefore began with Chrysler Corporation submitting a redesigned composite CHA front hull glacis incorporating the desired larger overhead hatches.

The Ordnance Department approved the Chrysler design in June 1943. However, at the same time, Fisher Body, a division of General Motors, submitted a superior ballistic design based on the M10 Tank Destroyer, which they had developed in early 1942.

The Fisher Body design consisted of a 63.5mm (2.5in) thick glacis sloped at 47 degrees, allowing for larger overhead hatches in the front roof of welded-hull Sherman tanks. The Ordnance Department quickly canceled the Chrysler design in favor of the Fisher Body design for all its welded-hull second-generation Sherman tanks.

The US Army officially referred to all Sherman tank components by their part numbers. For convenience, modelers and researchers have adopted the informal term 'large hatch' to describe second-generation 47-degree glacis-equipped Sherman tanks. The original first-generation Sherman tanks with the narrow hatches and 57-degree glacis are referred to as 'small hatch'. [The M4A4 never had the 47-degree glacis or large hatches fitted during production.]

New Suspension System

The complete range of second-generation upgrades did not appear on all Sherman tank production lines at the same time. An example was their suspension systems. Earlier-production second-generation tanks retained the original first-generation VVSS.

Later-manufactured second-generation tanks featured the new Horizontal Volute Spring Suspension (HVSS) system. Whereas the VVSS rode on tracks 16.5in wide, the HVSS system rode on 23in wide tracks. The HVSS system did improve the riding characteristics of the tanks, as well as their off-road flotation due to reduced ground pressure relative to VVSS.

The HVSS system for the second-generation Sherman tanks did impose a weight gain. The M4A1 (76) W riding on a VVSS weighed approximately 35 tons and, when riding on an HVSS system, around 37 tons. That weight gain shows up on tank data plates and can be employed to identify a tank riding on the HVSS system.

Of the 3,426 M4A1 (76) W built, 1,255 left the assembly line with the HVSS system. There is no substantial pictorial evidence to suggest that any fitted with the HVSS system saw combat in the ETO before the German surrender in May 1945.

Second-Generation M4A2s

A total of 2,915 M4A2 (76) W tanks came off the factory floor between May 1944 and May 1945. No official figures have yet surfaced, but estimates are that 1,594 examples appeared with VVSS and 1,321 with the HVSS system.

Overall, 2,073 M4A2 (76) W tanks went to the Soviet Union under Lend-Lease. Only five went to the United Kingdom. About 837 examples, riding on the HVSS system, were unallocated at the end of the Second World War and remained in the United States.

Transitional Features

Some late-production first-generation M4A2 tanks armed with a 75mm main gun left the factory in 1943 and 1944 with the new second-generation 47-degree reset glacis and the larger front hull hatches. However, they did not have the wet stowage ammunition arrangement of most second-generation Sherman tanks. A spotting feature of these tanks is their retention of welded-on armor plates on either side of their hulls over the ammunition stowage locations. Some of these tanks went to the Marine Corps.

Second-Generation M4A3s

A total of 4,542 examples of the M4A3 (76) W tanks came off the factory floor between March 1944 and April 1945. Of that number, 1,925 left the factory with the VVSS and 2,617 the HVSS system, with the first example with the HVSS coming down the assembly lines in August 1944.

The M4A3 (76) W tanks riding on the VVSS system began arriving in both the MTO and the ETO in late August 1944. Those built with the HVSS system began arriving in the ETO beginning in December 1944. Despite the improved flotation provided by the HVSS system, the harsh winter of 1944/45 in the ETO with the resulting heavy rain created enough mud to hamper even the HVSS system-equipped Sherman tanks.

75mm Gun-Armed Second-Generation Sherman

In addition to second-generation 76mm gun-armed versions of the M4A3, another 3,071 examples retained the 75mm main gun. These received the designation of 'M4A3 75mm Gun, Wet' on their data plates (for brevity's sake M4A3 (75) W), and rolled off the assembly lines from February 1944 through March 1945. Those built in 1944 came off the factory floor with the VVSS and those constructed in 1945 had the HVSS system.

The first examples of the M4A3 (75) W riding on the VVSS began arriving in the ETO sometime between July and August 1944. There is no

Suspension System Confusion

Much of the US Army wartime documentation on second-generation Sherman tanks does not differentiate between the types of suspension systems. According to the Sherman Minutia website, for production purposes, the Office of the Chief of Ordnance referred to Sherman tanks built with HVSS as 'wide track'. In some Army allocation and unit reports, this term is used, as well as '23in tracks'. However, there was no notation of the suspension type (VVSS or HVSS) on the original tank data plates.

The Ordnance Department assigned the HVSS system the experimental suffix 'E8', such as 'M4E8' or 'M4A3E8' and the term 'E8' does appear in some Second World War reports. However, 'M4A3E8' has come to be accepted by many as the official designation of the M4A3 with the 76mm gun and HVSS, probably as a result of the widespread use of the nickname 'Easy Eight' during the Korean War. The official designation that appears on the data plates of such tanks was 'Medium Tank, M4A3 76mm Gun, Wet'. Many writers (your author included) and researchers have taken to adding the designations VVSS and HVSS.

pictorial evidence to show that the M4A3 (75) W riding on the VVSS ever arrived in the MTO. None of the second-generation versions of the M4A3 went to Lend-Lease, as the M4A3 Medium Tank armed with either the 75mm or 76mm gun was the preferred tank of the US Army.

Unable to acquire additional first-generation M4A2 Medium Tanks from the US Army in 1945, the US Marine Corps took into service the M4A3 (75) W to supplement its remaining inventory of M4A2 Medium Tanks. Some Marine tank units preferred staying with the M4A2 Medium Tank, as they believed them to be safer when struck by anti-tank weapons due to diesel fuel's lower flammability. However, other Marine tankers wanted the new second-generation M4A3 (75) W tanks.

The rear bustle of the 75mm turret on the M4A3 (75) W tank was shifted up a few inches to provide clearance for the larger drivers' hatches hinges on second-generation hull designs. These turrets have been given the contemporary label 'high bustle' to distinguish them from the original 'low bustle' turret design.

The Muzzle Blast Problem

An issue that had concerned the Armored Board early on proved to be the 76mm gun's muzzle flash/blast, which blocked the tank commander's and gunner's view of the target effect in the crucial moments after firing.

From an August 1, 1952 Army report titled *A Survey of Tank Crew Problems*, there is this passage on the thoughts of a vehicle commander when firing the 76mm gun with his head above his cupola: 'The combination of the flash, concussion and flying metal from the rotating band make it difficult for the tank commander to accurately spot the hit of the round in order to make adjustments in the fire on the target.'

In the *United States vs. German Equipment* report of March 1945, Corporal Everette J. Harris made the observation:

Due to the type of powder a Jerry tank has, they can fire at you and are difficult to pick up because there is so little smoke or muzzle flash. When we fire our 76mm, there is so much smoke and muzzle flash that you can hardly observe your burst, except for long ranges.

Trying to Solve a Problem

The Ordnance Department dealt with the 76mm gun's excessive muzzle blast from two directions: reducing the smoke generated and controlling its spread. The amount of smoke was reduced by lengthening the powder fuze, providing a longer and more complete burn of the propellant. By controlling the spread, the smoke generated would be moved out of the line of sight to the target, using a muzzle brake, which diverted the smoke to either side of the barrel. The muzzle end of the barrel was threaded, to accept the muzzle brake. The redesigned gun with threaded barrel-end was designated 76mm Gun M1A1C, with a thread protector installed until the muzzle brakes were available. These were ready by July 1944. The complete configuration was designated the 76mm Gun M1A2.

A quote by Major Paul A. Bane, Jr appears in the 2nd Armored Division report of March 1945 titled *United States vs. German Equipment*. He stated that his units had just received some M4A3 tanks, armed with the 76mm gun, fitted with muzzle brakes: 'Test firing and combat operations have proven the muzzle brake to be a great help. We consider muzzle brakes an essential part of the tank gun.'

105mm Howitzer-Armed Sherman Tank

Included in the second-generation line-up would be two models armed with a 105mm howitzer: the M4 and M4A3. However, they were not fitted with wet stowage as were the other second-generation Sherman tanks. In a US Army manual dated September 8, 1944 titled *Assault Gun Section and Platoon* is this passage describing their intended role:

The primary mission of the assault gun is to give close fire support to small units [armor and armored infantry] battalion, company and platoon. In this role, it relieves the artillery of some close support missions but does not replace artillery fire. As a secondary mission, assault guns may be grouped and used as reinforcing artillery. Such missions must not interfere with their primary mission of close support.

The lack of wet stowage on these 105mm howitzer-armed Sherman tanks was over time increasingly risky in combat. General Roderick R. Allen, commanding general of the 12th Armored Division, wrote:

> In the Colmar action we had three armored vehicles – an M4A3 assault gun 105, an M4A3-76 and an M4A3E8 – hit at about the same place and in the same manner by concealed German guns. The assault tank [gun] disintegrated, and the M4A3-76 burned. The M4A3E8 was penetrated but did not burn or blow up due to the armor-plating, which protects the ammunition racks. The E8 was repaired and back in action in twenty-four hours.

A total of 3,039 examples of the M4A3 (105) and 1,641 examples of the M4 (105) left the factory floor between February 1944 and June 1945. The M4A3 (105) served only in the US Army, whereas 593 examples of the M4 (105) went to the British Army through Lend-Lease. About half of the howitzer-armed tanks built rode on the HVSS system.

Not Wanted or Needed

On the arrival of the first batch of 130 examples of the M4A1 (76) W tanks, riding on the VVSS, in England in April 1944, a firepower demonstration took place to show off the new tank to senior US Army officers. However, rather than encouraging the audience to embrace the better-armed tank, the opposite occurred. The officers felt that the gun design had not yet reached maturity, and therefore saw it as a troublesome fix for a mere inch of additional armor penetration.

Their concerns revolved around re-training tankers on the new gun, as well as the added logistical burden it would impose on the US Army as it prepared to invade occupied France. Another was the Army's unfounded confidence in tank destroyers, whether towed or self-propelled. Officers in Eisenhower's HQ – General Patton and the First United States Army Group's (FUSAG's) senior officers – tried again shortly after D-Day, but the results were the same.

A Different View

Army tankers were confident that their first-generation Sherman tank could deal with German late-war tanks, as they had in Italy. Their attitude was in part due to the small number of German tanks encountered, especially Panthers and Tigers. The German tanks encountered were hampered by terrain, poor tactical employment and the abysmal weather, especially mud, adding to American over-confidence.

Yet despite American confidence, the *Report of the New Weapon Board*, released in April 1944 and based on interviews conducted in the MTO, included this statement: 'There is an overwhelming demand for 76mm guns in M4 tanks.' This need was the result of US Army tankers' encounters with German Mark IV Medium Tanks' longer-ranged and more potent 75mm guns, as well as German 75mm towed anti-tank guns.

Painful Surprise

Once the US Army pushed inland after D-Day (June 6, 1944), it encountered the vast expanse of Normandy's hedgerow country. Unfortunately, Allied planners had not foreseen just how much of a terrain obstacle this posed and the defensive advantage it provided to the enemy.

Even worse, US Army tankers began encountering Panther tanks. The first extensive occasion occurred on July 8, 1944. The Panthers' thick frontal armor proved impervious to first-generation M4 and M4A1 tanks' 75mm main guns, except at point-blank range. This bitter truth was confirmed just two days later with firing trials conducted with a knocked-out Panther tank. The only US Army weapons that could penetrate the Panther glacis plate – and only at short ranges – were the towed 105mm howitzer and the towed M-1A 90mm anti-aircraft gun.

American tank losses, not just to Panther tanks but other enemy weapons as well, greatly exceeded what US planners had anticipated, resulting in a shortage of Sherman tanks and higher Army tanker casualties, requiring more trained replacements. British Army tank losses during the same period were even higher, as OVERLORD strategy called for the British to face the bulk of German armored formations contesting the invasion.

Too Late to do Any Good

The reason behind this was a significant failure of analysis, both from a lack of information as well as using US Army frameworks to estimate German intentions. The Ordnance Department had received Soviet intelligence about the Panther, but clearly discounted the threat it posed, possibly reflecting an attitude about the source. It never asked to inspect those captured by the Soviets. The Ordnance Department had only just learned before OVERLORD that the Panther was the planned replacement for the Mark IV Medium Tank series. The Ordnance Department had previously believed the Panther to be simply another heavy tank like the Tiger I, built in small numbers and employed at the corps level for special operations.

The Armored Force had figured out by the spring of 1944 that the Panther tank would pose a much more severe threat than previously thought. The AGF therefore suggested in an April 17, 1944 report that it would require what they referred to as a 'fighter tank' to deal with the Panther.

The April 17th letter stated: 'Available information on characteristics of German tanks compared to those of our nation show that no American tank can equal the German Panther in all-around performance.' However, it was then too late to do anything about it, for any new or modified American-designed tank would reach the field by the summer of 1944. If decisions had been made in 1943, there might have been a much better chance of having the so-called fighter tank.

Looking for a Solution

The sad news of the inferiority of first-generation Sherman tanks traveled up the chain of command to General Dwight D. Eisenhower, Supreme Commander of the Allied Expeditionary Forces in Europe (SHAEF). On July 2, 1944 he complained to the Ordnance Department officers on his staff about the matter. They, in turn, asked their counterparts in the United States for a quick solution, but none was at hand.

Eisenhower then sent Brigadier General Joseph A. Holly, Chief of the Armor Section for the ETO, back to the United States with a letter for General George S. Marshall, US Army Chief of Staff. The letter asked for 90mm-gun-armed tanks and tank destroyers to be shipped to the ETO as soon as possible.

While in the United States, Holly had a chance to see the single experimental M4A3 Sherman tank armed with the desired 90mm main gun. His interest in the vehicle as a quick solution to Eisenhower's firepower problem went nowhere. Ordnance Department representatives on site informed him that it would take approximately six months for production of the tank to ramp up. By that time, they told him, a new 90mm-gun-armed tank (which eventually became the M26 Heavy Tank) would be coming off the factory floor.

Give Us What You Got

In the meantime, a hue and cry went out for the unwanted M4A1 (76) W VVSS tanks, which were in storage in England. In mid-July 1944, General Omar N. Bradley, commander of the First Army, had 102 of them transported to the Normandy beachhead to support Operation COBRA, scheduled to begin on July 25. The offensive, based on the tremendous capability of the greatly-motorized Allied forces, proved to be hugely successful, breaking open the German lines and opening a gateway to all of Northern France. It led to the relatively quick collapse of opposing German forces in France and the encirclement of most of the divisions opposing the beachhead. The impact of the M4A1 (76) W was likely small, given its limited numbers.

Despite Operation COBRA's triumph, there remained a troublesome issue with the 76mm-gun-armed Sherman tanks involved. To everybody's surprise, their main gun proved unable to penetrate the frontal armor of the Panther tank (except for the Panthers' gun shield at 200 yards or less on occasion).

Eisenhower commented, 'You mean our 76 won't knock these Panthers out? Why, I thought it was going to be the wonder gun of the war.' Bradley responded that 'this new weapon often scuffed rather than penetrated the enemy's armor.'

In the March 1945 report titled *United States vs. German Equipment* is a quote by Sergeant John S. Banfield: 'We came in contact with a German Mark V and at a range of 70 yards, our 76mm gun would not penetrate the front plate.' In the same report, tank driver Delbert C. Grimmett commented: 'I saw an American 76mm on an M4 shoot a German Mark V at a range of 100 feet in the gun shield and not penetrate over two inches.'

Somebody Screwed Up

The Ordnance Department's wildly optimistic claims for the 76mm gun's armor penetration capabilities was the result of an unrealistic testing process. Instead of trying to recreate the same hard and well-sloped quality armor plate found on actual Panther tanks, the Ordnance Department used the softer armor plate developed for American tanks and fired at near-vertical plates.

The Advantage of Sloped Armor

An explanation of sloped armor's advantage appeared on March 21, 1950 in the US Army report titled *The Vulnerability of Armored Vehicles to Ballistic Attack*: 'An invulnerable frontal area will increase a vehicle's chance of survival, significantly. Tests made by the British show that for best protection against APC projectiles, the armor obliquity should be between 50 and 70 degrees with a preference nearer to 50 than 70 degrees.' Panther glacis armor had a slope of 55 degrees.

Armor sloped at certain angles effectively doubles the armor protection of a given thickness. Unfortunately, to account for this, the Ordnance Department used what turned out to be a very flawed mathematical formula. It also did not make allowances for the fact that AP projectiles often ricocheted off well-sloped armor plate.

Tank Mounted 17-Pounder Gun

In January 1944, the British Army demonstrated its new 17-pounder-armed Sherman tank to senior US Army officers. They also offered the design to the US Army. The American officers were not impressed with the up-armed tank and criticized some of its design features.

There were several reasons for rejecting the 17-pounder-armed Sherman tank. First, it would have taken two years for American industry to mass-produce the gun's ammunition and British industry hadn't the capacity to produce enough 17-pounder ammunition for both armies. Second, the US Army had already begun production of its 76mm and 90mm guns, as well as the needed ammunition. Third, the US Army remained convinced that its 76mm and 90mm guns, firing a new soon-to-be-fielded type of AP round, were equal in performance to the 17-pounder gun.

More Details

The British modified three versions of first-generation Sherman tanks to mount the 17-pounder gun. These included the M4 with the standard RHA upper hull, the M4 with the composite upper hull and the M4A4. The corresponding official British Army designations were the IC (Roman numeral 1 and C), IC Hybrid and VC (5-C). Approximately 2,000 examples of the various 17-pounder Shermans came off the factory floor between January 1944 and May 1945.

The unofficial nickname for all three up-armed Sherman tanks was 'Firefly'. That name does not show up in any official British Army wartime documents but appears in unit diaries. Other unofficial nicknames include 'Sherman 17-pounder' or just '17-pounder tank'.

The Good and the Bad Points

The Firefly's AP round contained a great deal more propellant than its American 76mm counterpart and almost as much as the US Army 90mm AP rounds. It offered superior armor penetration compared to all the American tank rounds. However, the 17-pounder's accuracy sometimes suffered, attributed to quality control issues during manufacture.

The downside of all the propellant in the 17-pounder's cartridge case was that when fired, the gun generated a massive muzzle blast, which despite the gun's muzzle brake, obscured the target momentarily. That drawback, and others, was acceptable to the British Army as the Firefly existed only as a stopgap vehicle.

Montgomery wrote in a 1944 letter, 'The 17-Pdr tank is most popular. The crews consider themselves a match for any German tank.' Despite its reputation as a tank-killer, the 17-pounder gun did not always guarantee a kill every time. An example appears in a post-war history of the 23rd Hussars: 'The 17-pounder was more encouraging ... for it penetrated the front of the Panther's turret at 300 yards, though it did not always go through the sloped front plate of the hull. On the whole, we decided that head-on Panthers should be treated with circumspection.'

Change of Heart

With a pressing need for a tank armed with a gun that could penetrate the Panther's frontal armor, the US Army's senior officers' previous negative opinions regarding the Firefly vanished. On August 9, 1944 Bradley asked Field Marshal Bernard Montgomery if it would be possible to acquire the Firefly.

Montgomery informed Bradley that if he wanted Fireflies, he would have to supply his tanks as the British Army then had a shortage due to heavy combat losses. The same problem bedeviled the US Army in France, worsened by cutbacks in production by American factories due to a faulty belief that war in the ETO would end fairly quickly.

In early 1945, the US Army supplied the British Army with 160 examples of first-generation Sherman tanks, both M4 and M4A3s Medium Tanks to convert to the 17-pounder configuration at British factories. Only 100 were completed, with eighty delivered to the US Army in the ETO. However, they arrived too late to see combat. The US Army told the British Army to retain the remaining twenty converted tanks, as well as the sixty unconverted tanks.

A dozen British Army Fireflies from their stockpiles in Italy went to a US Army tank company in early 1944, but they never saw combat.

New Ammunition

On August 19, 1944 three Panther tanks in varying stages of disrepair were brought together in France for another test of US Army anti-tank weapon effectiveness. On this occasion, the Ordnance Department brought along its new 76mm Hyper Velocity Armor Piercing (HVAP) round. A description of that round appears in a September 1950 US Army report titled *The Vulnerability of Armored Vehicles to Ballistic Attack*: 'The HVAP projectile consists of an extremely hard tungsten carbide core contained within an outer aluminum carrier with a windshield attached to the nose … The tungsten carbide core has almost twice the density of steel … and therefore, at the same velocity, has almost twice the kinetic energy.'

Despite everybody's high expectations for the HVAP round, which had a muzzle velocity of 3,400 ft per second, it failed to penetrate the glacis of the assembled Panther tanks. It did, however, demonstrate that it could penetrate other areas of the German tanks.

In an August 30, 1944 document titled *Final Report of Board of Officers appointed to Determine Comparative Effectiveness of Ammunition of 76mm Gun and 17-pdr Gun* is this passage from the concluding section of the report:

> That the 17-pdr APCBC and the 76mm HVAP, T4 are considered the best anti-tank ammunition available in these calibers for use against heavy armor. The 17-pdr APCBC is somewhat superior to the 76mm HVAP, T4 against the Panther tank. Neither one can be depended upon to penetrate the glacis plate of the Panther in one fair hit on average-quality plate.

From the March 1945 2nd Armored Division report *United States vs. German Equipment* is a quote by Colonel Paul A. Disney: 'When engaged at close range with HVAP, 76mm guns have disabled German tanks, but penetration of armor seems to be rare.'

How to Overcome the Enemy's Range Advantage

In May 1983, Colonel (retired) James H. Leach returned to the US Armor School to answer faculty questions they had posed regarding his time with the 4th Armored Division during the Second World War. One of the questions asked was what tactics did the M4 tanks use to close with German Panther tanks at longer ranges?

> The 'smoke' round, both tank and artillery, was the key to combating the tough Panther over open terrain. The WP was frequently the first round out the tube of the 75mm gun. Unfortunately, we had no 76mm smoke, which caused me to keep at least one old 75mm Sherman in each platoon so we could have readily available smoke to accomplish our missions. The WP provided three advantages: (1) mark targets; (2) kill targets; and (3) screen friendly forces.
>
> Artillery preparations, including smoke, were held on enemy positions as the US massed tanks moved as 'ships on the sea' toward the enemy. Artillery was only lifted as we closed on the position. Point targets were quickly engaged by tanks with smoke, HE or shot.

In the same report, Lieutenant Colonel Wilson M. Hawkins stated: 'Some of my tank crews claim penetrations on the front plate of Mark V tanks, using the 76mm gun and HVAP ammunition ... So far, however, we have never been able to supply a tank with more than two or three rounds of this ammunition.' The shortage of HVAP rounds persisted to the end of the war in the ETO.

Up-Armored Sherman Tanks

In late 1943, in consideration of the impending invasion of the Continent, the AGF began thinking about a very heavily-armored tank to support infantry divisions. It was assumed that it would be the T26E1, which eventually developed into the M26 Heavy Tank.

As it became clear that the M26 Heavy Tank would not be ready for the invasion of the Continent in summer of 1944, attention in December 1943 turned to an up-armored Sherman tank. The result was the authorization of 5 pre-production pilots and 254 production examples of the M4A3E2 Assault Tank. The term 'assault tank' appeared on their data plates.

Production of the M4A3E2 began in May and ended in July 1944, with the first examples arriving in the ETO in the fall of 1944. The extra armor brought the M4A3E2 up to 42 tons. An unofficial and popular nickname for the M4A3E2 that first appeared in the Second World War is 'Jumbo'.

The M4A3E2 consisted of a second-generation M4A3 (75) W tank, minus the VVSS system and wet stowage. It had an additional 38mm (1.5in) of RHA welded onto the existing glacis plate and upper hull sides. The lower hull and top armor were not up-armored. A new, much thicker CHA final drive housing was also applied. The M4A3E2 received an up-armored second-generation 76mm-armed CHA turret with its sides 152mm (6in) thick and a CHA gun shield 178mm (7in) thick.

Positive Impressions

Although initially seen as an infantry division support vehicle, many of the M4A3E2 tanks went to armored divisions in the ETO. They employed them as point tanks since their extra armor could sometimes deflect the AP projectiles fired by German anti-tank guns, waiting in ambush.

From a 12th Army Group Report of Operations is this extract: 'These tanks [M4A3E2s] ... were amazingly successful in operation, taking punishment not possible with the standard M4 series tanks. In spite of the increased weight, no extra suspension troubles occurred, and the campaign ended with many of these tanks still in operation.'

Such was the M4A3E2's popularity in the ETO that Eisenhower sent a message to the War Department on January 31, 1945 asking for an improved version of the tank armed with a 76mm main gun and riding on an HVSS system. As production of what became the Pershing had already begun and deliveries to the ETO were expected soon, Eisenhower's request went nowhere. One can only wonder their impact if 1,000 examples had shown up to see service in the ETO.

Beginning in February 1945, approximately 100 of the Third Army's M4A3E2 tanks were up-armed with a 76mm main gun. As initially envisioned, the M4A3E2 was to have a 76mm main gun. Early on, that changed to a 75mm main gun, with the thought in mind that as an infantry support weapon, the superior 75mm HE round would make more sense than the 76mm's inferior HE round.

Improvised M4A3E2 Tanks

The Third Army's answer to the shortage of M4A3E2 tanks involved cutting the RHA plates off derelict American and German tanks and welding them onto existing M4A3 (76) W tanks on the HVSS system. There is also pictorial evidence that some First Army M4A3 (76) W tanks, riding on the HVSS system, adopted the Third Army practice.

Besides the M4A3 (76) W with the HVSS system, earlier-production examples riding on the VVSS appear in wartime images with welded-on extra armor. There are also pictures from the ETO showing other versions of the second-generation Sherman tanks fitted with extra armor.

Surprise, Surprise

By the late fall of 1944, consensus arose among US Army senior-level leadership in the ETO that Germany would soon collapse. With that thought in mind, there was little concern about the Sherman tank's shortcomings, demonstrated so clearly in the early summer of 1944. Hitler, however, had a surprise for the Western Allies, code-named *Unternehmen Wacht am Rhein* (Operation Watch on the Rhine), which he launched on December 16, 1944.

To Americans, the fierce battles fought in the Ardennes Forest of Belgium and Luxembourg between December 1944 and January 1945 were better known as 'the Battle of the Bulge'. In the end, the US Army repulsed the German offensive. It then pushed the German Army back to its original starting positions by mid-January 1945, inflicting heavy losses in men and equipment on the enemy.

Numbers

The cost to the US Army in throwing back the German offensive operation was too high, not just in personnel but in equipment such as tanks. From

A Dead End

Before the M4A3E2 tank, the Ordnance Department, in conjunction with the British Tank Mission to the United States, had given some thought to a heavily-armored infantry support assault tank.

An agreement was reached that both American and British industry would build two pilots for testing, the Americans using a much-modified first-generation Sherman tank and the British their Mark VIII Cruiser tank. The better-performing prototype would go into production. The British Army estimated that it would require 8,500 examples of the winning tank.

The Ordnance Committee issued specifications for the American version in May 1942 and designated it the T14 Assault Tank. One of the two pilots was available for testing in July 1942 and the second pilot appeared the following month.

The pilot tanks featured 101mm (4in) of armor on their glacis, with their CHA turrets ranging in thickness from 76mm to 101mm. Armor on the remainder of the vehicle greatly exceeded that of the standard first-generation Sherman. The weight came in at 47 tons, with the vehicles riding on an early version of the HVSS system using M6 Heavy Tank tracks.

Testing proved unsatisfactory, with many unresolved design shortcomings. The Armored Force had no interest in the concept and work ground to a halt. Official cancelation occurred on December 14, 1944.

November 20, 1944 to January 20, 1945, the US Army lost 1,080 Sherman tanks, including both the 75mm- and 76mm-armed versions. One US Army divisional commander wished for better-armed tanks 'prayerfully or profanely – wherever the enemy panzer divisions appeared out of the Ardennes hills and forests.'

During the Battle of the Bulge, the 75mm-gun-armed versions of the Sherman tank continued to outnumber the 76mm-gun-armed models. In November 1944, records show the US Army's armored divisions in the ETO had 1,041 of the 75mm-gun-armed Sherman tanks and only 239 of their 76mm counterparts.

Continued deliveries and repair depots worked steadily to recover the losses. As of February 1945, the percentage of 76mm-gun-armed Sherman tanks in General Omar Bradley's 12th Army Group represented more than a quarter of its medium tank inventory. By the time of the German surrender in early May 1945, these Shermans constituted almost half of the medium tanks then in service.

A Re-Run

As the US Army went on the defensive during the early part of the Battle of the Bulge, they did enjoy a slight advantage. However, the better-armed and armored German tanks such as the Panther, of which they had 341 examples along with 66 Tiger tanks, led to some uneven engagements in which the Sherman tanks took heavy losses, as they had in France in June and July 1944.

Lieutenant Colonel Matthew E. Kane of the 3rd Armored Division complained about the uneven odds between the Sherman tank and the late-war German tanks:

> . . . and our tank losses in the Belgian Bulge were relatively high, even when we were in defensive positions. Crews recognized the deficiencies in our tanks, and knew that success on the battlefield is attributable to our superiority in numbers and tanks, and resolved to sustain heavy casualties in men in tanks in order to gain objectives.

No More 75mm Gun-Armed Sherman Tanks

Following the Battle of the Bulge, to make up for the large number of tanks lost, the Army's front-line armor commanders stated that they wanted no more 75mm gun-armed Sherman tanks. Eisenhower himself notified the War Department in January 1945 that he only wanted Sherman tanks armed with the 76mm gun. According to the US Army's official history of the Second World War, in the volume titled *On Beachhead and Battlefront*:

> When Colonel [Joseph M.] Colby [of the Ordnance Department] tried to sell the battalion commanders of the 3d Armored Division on the

---

Improvised Artillery

On occasion, first-generation Sherman tanks armed with 75mm main guns were employed as self-propelled artillery in both the MTO and ETO. An example of that appears in a post-war research report from the Armored School, dated June 1949 and titled *Armor Under Adverse Conditions: 2nd and 3rd Armored Divisions in the Ardennes Campaign*:

> Allied tanks . . . were also used as artillery. They were shuttled from place to place, where fire support was needed by troops holding Allied front lines . . . all tankers were taught artillery methods of fire control and support. They learned to elevate the tank tracks on logs, or on the banks of the many drainage ditches present in the area, to get the desired or required targets. This was to supplement artillery fire, which at one time was limited by short supply of ammunition.

Shermans they already had (being unable to offer them anything better on a large scale immediately), he ran into a hornet's nest. After the heavy casualties of the winter, they were beginning to regard the 75mm Shermans as deathtraps.

The Press Gets Involved

The low morale among many American tankers regarding the uneven odds they faced in battle with German tanks caught the attention of the American Press Corps. Both Hanson W. Baldwin, the military editor of the *New York Times*, and Eugene Meyer, the editor of the *Washington Post*, questioned in early 1945 articles why at that late stage of the war, American tanks continued to remain inferior to their German counterparts.

Baldwin wrote in a January 5, 1945 article titled 'New German Tanks Prove Superior to Ours – Inquiry by Congress Urged':

Why at this late stage in the war are American tanks inferior to the enemy's? That they are inferior the fighting in Normandy showed, and the recent battles in the Ardennes have again emphatically demonstrated. This has been denied, explained away and hushed up, but the men who are fighting our tanks against much heavier, better-armored and more powerfully-armed German monsters know the truth. It is high time that Congress got at the bottom of a situation that does no credit to the War Department.

The *Washington Post* editor wrote in the March 22, 1945 edition of the newspaper: 'It is scandalous that this lag should have been allowed. This country prides itself on its incomparable industrial and engineering genius. Yet it has fallen behind both our Russian ally and our Nazi enemy in arming the ground forces with their basic weapon [the tank].'

Denial

When questioned during a March 1945 press conference about the negative articles regarding the inferiority of American tanks, Patton defended the tanks, as could be expected, fearful of the negative effect it would have on the tankers and those building the tanks. At that point, the US Army's senior leadership launched a public relations campaign to prevent the American public from becoming too alarmed.

Part of the Army's public relations campaign involved releasing a letter Patton had written to another general in which he criticized 'certain misguided or perhaps mendacious individuals who criticize American tanks'. During another press conference, Patton stated, without any statistical proof, that 'our tanks had destroyed twice as many German tanks as

American forces had lost'. He then added '... that all of our equipment, clothing, etc. was superior to anything the Allies or the German had.'

The Opinion of Tankers

In the March 21, 1945 report *United States vs. German Equipment* is the following quote by Lieutenant General John H. Collier: 'In my opinion, press reports of statements by high-ranking officers to the effect that we have the best equipment in the world do much to discourage the soldier who is using equipment that he knows to be inferior to that of the enemy.'

Eisenhower wrote to the Army Chief of Staff, General George C. Marshall, on March 26, 1945 that, with the exception of German tanks, 'only the German bazooka may be considered superior to an item of ours.'

In a book titled *Move Out, Verify: The Combat Story of the 743rd Tank Battalion* is a passage describing a conversation among the unit's tankers. Somebody mentioned that a particular tank general had claimed that '... the Sherman was better than the German tanks because of speed, maneuverability and reliability.' The answer from another tanker present: 'Better, Hell! The only thing we have over the Germans is that we've got more tanks and build more, faster. And that's a comfortable thought for a guy when a Mark VI [Tiger] starts shooting at him, isn't it?'

A buck sergeant continued, commenting: 'I would use diesel engines so that there wouldn't be any high-test gasoline and its fumes to make an incendiary bomb out of my buggy [tank].'

The Ordnance Department began thinking ahead about an improved M4 series tank even before the first M4 production example came off the factory floor. Pictured here is an artist's concept of an improved M4 series tank. However, several design flaws such as the main gun rounds stored in the upper hull sides (sponsons) and having the fuel tanks at the bottom of the hull meant that it never left the drawing board. (*Patton Museum*)

What Received Praise After the War?

Upon the conclusion of the Second World War, some US Army generals made comments on the equipment employed. Devers, who had played an essential role in the development of the Sherman tank, commented with a less than ringing endorsement that '. . . the Sherman did the job'.

What were Patton's true feelings about American tanks? Shortly after the war, he stated: 'I don't have to tell you who won the war, you know our artillery did.' Eisenhower also failed to mention American tanks. Instead he, like Patton, praised the artillery: 'The speed, accuracy and devastating power of American artillery won confidence and admiration from the troops it supported and inspired fear and respect in their enemy.'

Initial consideration of an up-armed M4 series tank resulted in an early-production M4A1 Medium Tank armed with the 76mm (76.2mm) Gun T1 as seen here. As the barrel's length and weight caused the turret to be badly out of balance, 15in of the barrel were cut off to reduce the imbalance. The Ordnance Department saw promise with the concept and proceeded with its development. (*Patton Museum*)

The next step in developing a 76mm gun-armed M4 series tank involved the construction of additional M4A1 Medium Tanks armed with the 76mm (76.2mm) Gun T1, now standardized as the M1. The vehicles so armed became the Medium Tank M4A1 (76M1), with an example pictured here. The Ordnance Department liked the result and wanted 1,000 of them built. The Armored Force told the Ordnance Department 'no' until they had the opportunity to test it. (*Patton Museum*)

The Armored Board's testing of the M4A1 (76M1) led it to conclude that the existing turret proved too small for the crew to operate efficiently. Hence the tank proved unacceptable to them. The next iteration involved adding a larger turret design based on the never-fielded M23 Medium Tank turret. That larger turret design went onto an M4 composite hull tank as pictured here. The combination became the M4E6. (*Patton Museum*)

The Armored Board liked what they saw with the M4E6, prompting the Army Ground Forces (AGF) to request 1,000 examples. At the same time, the AGF stated that when production of the M4E6 began, it wanted to end production of the first-generation M4 series tanks armed with the 75mm gun. The Armored Force wanted to keep the first-generation M4 series tanks in production as they fired a superior HE round. (*Patton Museum*)

Rather than using the M4 composite hull armed with the 76mm gun-armed turret, as had the M4E6, production examples employed the upgraded M4A1, M4A2 and M4A3 hulls, with second-generation features. Pictured here is an M4A1 (76) W, riding on the first-generation VVSS system. Production began in January 1944. (*Pierre-Olivier Buan*)

(**Above**) Pictured here is the thirty-seventh example built of the M4A1 (76) W, riding on the VVSS system and nicknamed 'the Gila Monster'. Note the vehicle commander has the 'Cupola, Commander's Vision'. The loader's hatch is the former split hatch for the vehicle commander's position on first-generation M4 series tanks. Eventually, the loader's split hatch would disappear, replaced by a new oval hatch on second-generation M4 series tanks. (*National Archives*)

(**Opposite, above**) Unlike the Combination Gun Mount M34A1, which consisted of a gun shield and rotor shield, the second-generation M4 medium tanks armed with the 76mm gun featured a single-piece, full-width gun shield with a thickness of 89mm (3.5in) as seen here. The new gun shield bore the designation of Gun Mount M62. (*Pierre-Olivier Buan*)

(**Opposite, below**) An external design feature of the M4 series tanks armed with the 76mm gun was a reset glacis with a 47-degree slope. That design change did away with the need for hatch hoods, as seen on this M4A3 (76) W. The reset of the glacis on the M4A1 (76) W is less noticeable due to its more contoured hull shape. (*Pierre-Olivier Buan*)

(**Above**) To offset the reduction of ballistic protection with a more vertically-sloped glacis on second-generation M4 series tanks, their glacis was thickened to 63.5mm (2.5in). To improve the protection level of their hull armor, many first- and second-generation M4 series tankers in the ETO began adding sandbags, starting in the summer of 1944. Pictured here is a heavily-sandbagged M4A3 (76) W. (*Patton Museum*)

(**Opposite, above**) The front hull hatches on an M4A3 (76) W. Note the welded steel rod guards over the rotating periscopes, a common feature found on late-production first-generation M4 series tanks and most second-generation M4 series tanks. Both the driver and bow gunner also have fixed forward periscopes, as seen here. Between the two hatches is the upper portion of an electric-powered ventilator. (*Pierre-Olivier Buan*)

(**Opposite, below**) From a wartime manual comes this illustration of the components that made up the 76mm Tank Gun. The gun itself came in multiple versions, including the M1, the M1A1 and the last model, the M1A2. Eventually, the M1A1 and M1A2 had a 62lb muzzle brake fitted, which began showing up in July 1944. (*Patton Museum*)

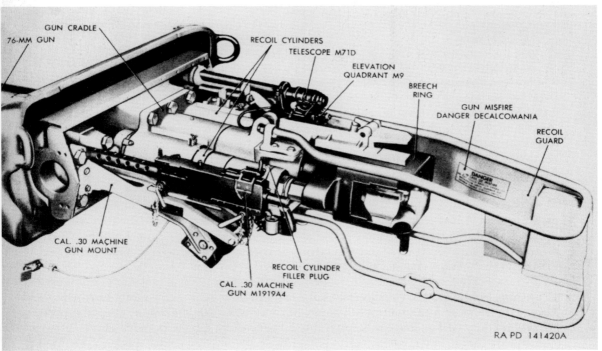

76-MM GUN
GUN CRADLE
RECOIL CYLINDERS
TELESCOPE M71D
ELEVATION QUADRANT M9
BREECH RING
GUN MISFIRE DANGER DECALCOMANIA
RECOIL GUARD
DANGER
CAL. .30 MACHINE GUN MOUNT
RECOIL CYLINDER FILLER PLUG
CAL. .30 MACHINE GUN M1919A4

RA PD 141420A

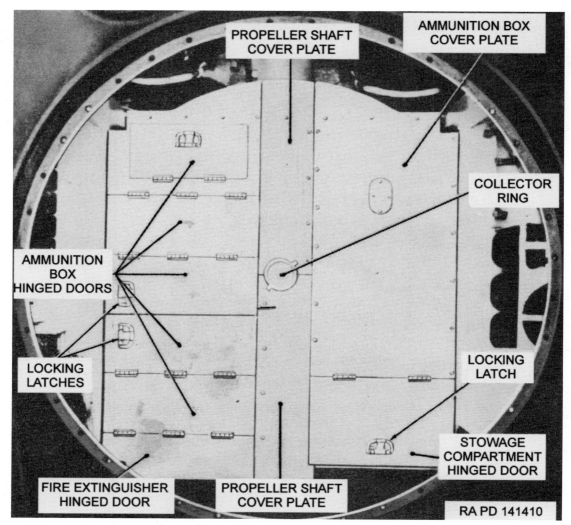

PROPELLER SHAFT
COVER PLATE

AMMUNITION BOX
COVER PLATE

COLLECTOR
RING

AMMUNITION
BOX
HINGED DOORS

LOCKING
LATCHES

LOCKING
LATCH

STOWAGE
COMPARTMENT
HINGED DOOR

FIRE EXTINGUISHER
HINGED DOOR

PROPELLER SHAFT
COVER PLATE

RA PD 141410

(**Above**) To reduce vulnerability of the second-generation 76mm gun-armed M4 series tanks to ammunition fires, all their main gun rounds went into compartments in the lower hull. Of the authorized seventy-one rounds, thirty-five were arrayed in five slanted rows, surrounded by liquid-filled containers, on the bottom of the tank's hull. They were below the turret basket, on the left-hand side of the hull, as seen in this illustration from a wartime manual. (*Patton Museum*)

(**Opposite, above**) Looking down the loader's hatch of a second-generation M4 series medium tank armed with a 76mm gun. The loader has opened a few of the hinged doors on the floor of his tank to display some of the main gun rounds stored within. Distribution of the various types of main gun rounds within the rack arrangement was left to the individual loader. (*National Archives*)

(**Opposite, below**) To provide access for the loader to the main gun rounds stored in the lower hull of second-generation M4 series tanks armed with the 76mm gun, the turret basket had only half its floor, as seen in this picture, looking back from the driver's seat. The armored box (center) on the turret basket floor and aligned under the gun contained six ready rounds. (*Pierre-Olivier Buan*)

(**Above**) Underneath the right-hand side of the turret basket floor of 76mm and 75mm gun-armed second-generation tanks with wet stowage resided the armored box pictured here, which contained room for thirty main gun rounds. In front of the ammunition storage box is the tank's bottom hull escape hatch. In front of the escape hatch would be the bow gunner's seat and back-rest, not pictured here. (*Pierre-Olivier Buan*)

(**Opposite, above**) Shown here is a size comparison between the two standard main gun rounds for the 75mm gun-armed M4 series tanks on the left and the standard armor-piercing (AP) round for the 76mm gun-armed second-generation M4 series tanks on the right. The muzzle velocity of the M62A1 AP round came out at 2,600fps. The complete round weighed about 27lb, with the projectile portion coming in at approximately 15lb. (*World War II Armor Museum*)

(**Opposite, below left**) In this labeled illustration we see the various components that made up the standard Armor-Piercing Capped-Tracer (APC-T) for both the 75mm and 76mm gun-armed M4 series medium tanks. The armor-piercing caps attached to the steel projectiles aided in overcoming FHA by protecting the main body of the projectile from shattering upon striking its target. (*James D. Brown*)

(**Opposite, below right**) Disappointment with the poor armor penetration capabilities of the Armor-Piercing Capped-Tracer (APC-T) M62A1 against German tanks led to the introduction of what eventually received the designation of the M93 High-Velocity Armor-Piercing-Tracer (HVAP-T) pictured here. Delivery to units in the field began in September 1944. (*World War II Armor Museum*)

75mm.
A.P.C. Shell, M61

75mm SHELL,
Fixed, H.E., M48

76mm
A.P.C. Shell, M62A1

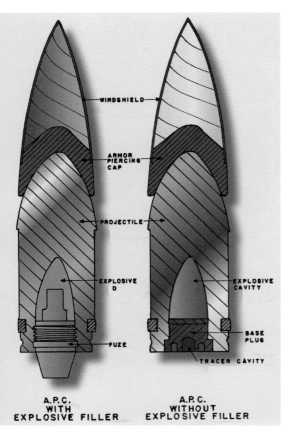

WINDSHIELD

ARMOR PIERCING CAP

PROJECTILE

EXPLOSIVE D

EXPLOSIVE CAVITY

FUZE

BASE PLUG

TRACER CAVITY

A.P.C.
WITH
EXPLOSIVE FILLER

A.P.C.
WITHOUT
EXPLOSIVE FILLER

This illustration shows the projectile portion of an M93 High-Velocity Armor-Piercing-Tracer (HVAP-T) round and labels its various components. Tank crews sometimes referred to the round as 'Hyper-Shot' to distinguish it from the standard AP rounds. (*James D. Brown*)

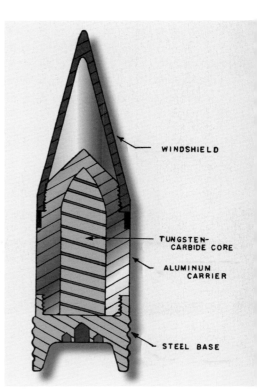

WINDSHIELD

TUNGSTEN-
CARBIDE CORE

ALUMINUM
CARRIER

STEEL BASE

The bow gunner's position in a 76mm gun-armed second-generation M4 series medium tank. To the right and directly above the breech end of the .30 caliber machine gun is the bottom portion of the loader's overhead hatch periscope. Seen to the left and above the machine gun is the lower portion of the loader's fixed overhead periscope. (*Chris Hughes*)

One of the major design changes that eventually appeared on the second-generation M4 series tanks was this new suspension system. Referred to as the Horizontal Volute Spring Suspension (HVSS) system, it did much to resolve the problem of track-throwing that plagued M4 series tanks riding on the earlier VVSS system. (*Pierre-Olivier Buan*)

Pictured here is an M4A3 (76) W, with the HVSS system. The success of the new suspension system rested on several design features. One was the addition of shock absorbers, which the VVSS system lacked. Wider tracks required the use of dual bogies, thereby doubling their number, distributing their wear more uniformly than the individual bogies of the VVSS system. (*Pierre-Olivier Buan*)

TANK MEDIUM M 4A3 76 MM GUN, WET
ORDNANCE DEP'T., U.S. ARMY   SERIAL NO. 60035

M'F'D BY

CREW 5 MEN   FIGHTING WEIGHT 75900 LBS.
ENGINE CRUISING SPEED 2400 R.P.M.
MAX. FOR SHORT PERIODS 2600 R.P.M.
    PARTS LIST - ORD 9 SNL G205
OPERATOR'S MANUAL - TM. 9-759
MAINTENANCE MANUALS   9-1384   9-1731B   9-1731C
                         9-1750B   TB-9-1750K-2
9-1731G   9-1731K
        VEHICLE CRUISING SPEEDS -
                              5- 21 M.P.H.
1- 2 M.P.H.   3- 8 M.P.H.
2- 5 M.P.H.   4- 13 M.P.H.   REVERSE 3 M.P.H.

28 SEPT '49

(**Opposite, above**) Despite a great many tank buffs/modelers and even respected tank museums referring to the M4A3 (76) W riding on the HVSS system as the 'M4A3E8' or 'Easy Eight', that was not its designation, as seen on the data plate of one such tank. Neither M4A3E8 nor the name Easy Eight appears in any War Department wartime manuals. The Chief of Ordnance officially labeled those tanks with the HVSS system as 'wide track', but that never appeared on the tanks' data plates. (*Pierre-Olivier Buan*)

(**Opposite, below**) Construction of the M4A3 W, as pictured here, began in February 1944. By the time production ended in March 1945, approximately 3,000 examples had been built. It consisted of a second-generation hull, which included the reset and thickened 47-degree glacis as well as wet stowage but retained the 75mm gun and turret of the first-generation M4 series medium tanks. (*Pierre-Olivier Buan*)

(**Above**) The raised lugs of the new larger hatches that came along with the 47-degree second-generation glacis required a change in the turret. A new 75mm gun-armed turret was developed, with the raised rear bustle pictured here, which cleared the hatch lugs when the turret traversed. (*Pierre-Olivier Buan*)

(**Opposite, above**) Another view of the new 75mm gun-armed turret with the high bustle. The pistol port visible appeared on both first- and second-generation M4 series tanks. It proved a point of contention between the Ordnance Department and tank crews. Ordnance saw it as a ballistic weak spot and ordered it removed. The crews wanted it retained as an aid in loading the tank with main gun rounds and disposing of spent main gun cartridge cases. (*Pierre-Olivier Buan*)

(**Opposite, below**) Development of an M4 series medium tank armed with a 105mm howitzer had begun in early 1942. Two upgraded pilots, designated the M4E5, were built and delivered to the Aberdeen Proving Ground in August 1943 for testing by the Armored Board. Testing went well and the 105mm-armed turrets went onto the modified hulls of M4 and M4A3 Medium Tanks. The example pictured here is the M4 Medium Tank variant, armed with a 105mm howitzer. (*Pierre-Olivier Buan*)

(**Above**) Reflecting the 105mm howitzer's large size, the shape and the attachment points of the Combination Gun Mount M52 proved very different from the Combination Gun Mount M34A1 on the 75mm gun-armed M4 series tanks. The large opening seen on the left-hand side of the rotor shield proved vulnerable to small-arms fire and eventually resulted in the armored cover seen here that could be opened and closed from within the vehicle. (*Pierre-Olivier Buan*)

(**Above**) A soldier is pictured here passing a 105mm HE round to the loader inside a howitzer-armed M4 series medium tank by way of the pistol port. Instead of the fixed round fired by the 75mm and 76mm guns, 105mm rounds were semi-fixed. This means that the powder charge could be adjusted for the desired range by removing the projectile from its cartridge case prior to firing and inserting the required number of propellant charges based on range. (*Patton Museum*)

(**Opposite, above**) Pictured at an historical military vehicle demonstration is an M4A3 105mm riding on an HVSS system. The vehicle's data plate would read Tank Medium M4A3 105mm How. Both the M4 105mm and the M4A3 105mm had authorized storage for sixty-six rounds. The 105mm howitzer itself bore the designation M4. It weighed 1,140lb and had a length of around 8ft. (*World War II Armor Museum*)

(**Opposite, below**) The British Army had a much better awareness of the constant up-gunning and up-armoring of German tank designs. Dissatisfied with the 75mm gun's armor penetration, the British Army mounted its 17-pounder anti-tank guns on two different versions of the first-generation M4 series of medium tanks. These included the M4 and M4A4 Medium Tanks. Pictured here is an M4 Medium Tank with a composite hull and armed with a 17-pounder gun. (*Pierre-Olivier Buan*)

A

(**Opposite, above**) The vehicle commander of a 17-pounder-armed M4 series tank in the ETO. The British Army designation for the M4 Medium Tank with the 17-pounder was 'the Cruiser Tank Sherman IC' (Roman number 'I'), whereas the M4 Medium Tank with the composite hull became 'the IC Hybrid'. The M4A4 Medium Tank was 'the VC'. There were several unofficial nicknames for the tank, including 'the Sherman 17-pounder', 'the 17-pounder tank' and the best-known, 'the Firefly'. (*Tank Museum*)

(**Opposite, below**) Besides the 17-pounder gun's very long barrel and distinctive round muzzle brake, the most noticeable external feature of the Firefly was the armored box seen here. Welded to the turret bustle of the M4 and M4A4 series tanks, it contained the vehicle's No. 19 radio set. The radio had to be set back due to the 17-pounder gun's long recoil mechanism and breech. (*Tank Museum*)

(**Above**) The crew of a Firefly are shown in the process of loading their tank. The rounds' large size is clearly evident in the photograph. To provide maximum storage space for the tank's seventy-seven to seventy-eight main gun rounds, the bow gunner's position was done away with. In August 1944, there appeared the Armor-Piercing Discarding Sabot (APDS) round. It had a muzzle velocity of 3,950 ft per second (fps). (*Tank Museum*)

(**Above**) In early 1942, the US Army, as well as the British Tank Mission based in the United States, decided that a need existed for a heavily-armored assault tank. Both countries were to design a single prototype for consideration, with the superior model placed into production. As events transpired, neither country's submissions proved satisfactory. Pictured here is the American prototype designated the Assault Tank T14. (*Pierre-Olivier Buan*)

(**Opposite, above**) For the planned invasion of the Continent in the summer of 1944, the Ordnance Committee began thinking about the requirement for a heavily-armored assault tank in early 1944. As the Assault Tank T14 proved a design dead-end, a decision was made to up-armor 254 examples of the M4A3 Medium Tank, with the second-generation reset glacis as pictured here. The tanks received the designation M4A3E2. (*Pierre-Olivier Buan*)

(**Opposite, below**) The walls of the specially-designed CHA turret on the M4A3E2 Assault Tank had a thickness of 152mm (6in), as is evident in this picture. The T110 Combination Gun Mount had a thickness of 178mm (7in). Over the glacis of the M4A3 tank and the upper hull, an extra 38mm (1.5in) of RHA were welded on. The final drive assembly cover had a thickness of 140mm (5.5in). (*Pierre-Olivier Buan*)

(**Opposite, above**) Despite the impressive thickness of armor on the M4A3E2 Assault Tank, unofficially nicknamed 'the Jumbo', it was not immune to all the battlefield threats it would encounter, as this picture obviously suggests. Despite the second-generation reset front hull, the tank did not have wet stowage. Weight of the M4A3E2 came out at 44 tons, 7 tons more than the weight of an M4A3 (76) W riding on the HVSS system. (*National Archives*)

(**Opposite, below**) The popularity of the enhanced armor protection provided by the M4A3E2 and their limited number led to Patton's Third Army creating improvised versions, with an example pictured here. The extra armor came from knocked-out American and German tanks. The job of welding on the additional armor to the Third Army tanks went to two Belgian firms. The number of improvised M4A3E2 tanks fielded is unknown. (*National Archives*)

(**Above**) Besides up-armoring M4A3 second-generation M4A3 (76) W tanks, riding on the HVSS system, with armor plates cut off of destroyed tanks, the crew of this M4A1 (76) W riding on the VVSS have also added extra armor plate to the front hull of their tank. (*National Archives*)

Chapter Five

Tank Destroyers

The rapid, and unexpected fall of France in the summer of 1940 was attributed to a mistaken belief that hordes of German tanks had overwhelmed the French Army. The US Army, lacking an effective countermeasure, pursued a 1937 recommendation for specialized anti-tank units (later renamed tank destroyers) that would offensively seek out and destroy large formations of attacking German tanks.

The US Army, like the French Army before, founded its doctrine on towed anti-tank guns to halt enemy tank attacks – defensively or offensively. A corollary was to leave them free to maneuver: the Army's tanks should not be fighting its opponent's tanks except as a secondary mission. The primary purpose of tanks, Americans believed, was exploitation.

The Reasoning

Some of the doctrinal thinking behind the US Army's tank destroyers appeared in a July 1940 letter by Lieutenant General Lesley S. McNair, in which he stated it was 'poor economy to use a $35,000 medium tank to destroy another tank when the job can be done by a [towed] gun costing a fraction as much.' Simply put, economy was considered important: procurement, crew requirements, training, maintenance, shipping, etc.

Lieutenant General McNair proved to be the most influential proponent of tank destroyers. As the commanding general of the Army's General Headquarters (GHQ), which later became the Army Ground Force (AGF), his opinions carried a great deal of weight.

Lieutenant General McNair's faith in tank destroyers was seconded by Lieutenant Colonel Andrew D. Bruce, who eventually rose to the rank of lieutenant general. In March 1942 during an interview he stated:

> One good [towed] tank destroyer can be produced for materially less than a tank, and in far less time and with less critical materials. And by using tank destroyers to stop enemy tanks, you leave our tanks free to dash through and spread hell among the enemy.

General George C. Marshall, Army Chief of Staff, had assigned Lieutenant General Andrew Davis Bruce to lead and develop the Army's anti-tank force. The Tank Destroyer Tactical and Firing Center, located at Fort

George G. Meade, Maryland was transferred in March 1942 to the newly-constructed Camp Hood, Texas and re-designated as the 'Tank Destroyer Command' and subsequently the 'Tank Destroyer Center' in August 1942.

Self-Propelled

Lieutenant General McNair, who put a lot of faith in towed anti-tank guns, did not share Lieutenant General Andrew Davis Bruce's interest in self-propelled tank destroyers. He saw mobility as the key to a successful tank destroyer design. The importance of mobility for self-propelled tank destroyers appears in a War Department manual on the subject dated June 16, 1942:

> Rapidity of maneuver enables tank destroyer units to strike at vital objectives, fight on selected terrain, exercise pressure from varied and unexpected directions, and bring massed fire to bear in decisive areas. Tank destroyer units obtain results from rapidity and flexibility of action rather than by building up strongly-organized positions. Tank destroyers depend for protection not on armor, but on speed and the use of cover and terrain. When maneuvering in the presence of the enemy, they habitually move at the greatest speed permitted by the terrain.

American industry in 1942, already overwhelmed by the demands of an ever-enlarging US Army as well as other services, had no spare capacity to design and build a specialized tank destroyer for Lieutenant Colonel Andrew Davis Bruce. He, therefore, had to deploy several expedient tank destroyer designs until the ultimate tank destroyer could appear.

Half-Track Gun Motor Carriage

There was a wide variety of experimental tank destroyers developed and tested. The first, ordered into production on October 31, 1941, was the 75mm GMC (Gun Motor Carriage) T12. It consisted of a Half-Track, Personnel Carrier, M3, with a 75mm Gun M1897A4, better known to most at the time as the 'French 75'.

In the book *Faint Praise: American Tanks and Tank Destroyers during World War II* authored by Charles M. Baily appears the following passage that explains the development of the 75mm GMC T12:

> Inspiration for the M3 [75mm GMC T12] had come from a French designer who told Colonel Bruce [eventually head of the Tank Destroyer Command/Center] that the French Army had successfully mounted a 75mm on the back of trucks. The idea interested Bruce and

other members of the Planning Branch, who saw the US Army's new half-track personnel carrier [M3] at Aberdeen [Proving Ground, Maryland] a few days later. Soon after that, General Twaddle and Ordnance officers agreed to try out the mount.

The US Army adopted the French 75 in large numbers during the First World War. It remained in service during the interwar period along with American-built versions. On the M3 half-track, the French 75 was fitted onto a fixed forward-firing mount with limited traverse and elevation.

Into Service

The pilot example of the T12 appeared in the summer of 1941, with eighty-six production examples delivered between August and September 1941. Fifty were quickly shipped to the Philippines to bolster US Army forces stationed there. The remaining T12s were formed into a US-based anti-tank battalion for field testing. One finding from the trial was the need for a larger armored shield to improve protection for the gun crew.

The T12 was standardized in October 1941 as the Half-Track 75mm Gun Motor Carriage [GMC] M3. An improved version, including the improved crew shield, received the designation M3A1. Between February 1942 and February 1943, a total of 2,030 examples of the M3/M3A1 tank GMC came off the assembly lines.

The half-track-based tank destroyers saw action in North Africa from December 1942 until May 1943, when they were pulled from front-line service. They would linger on in some rear-echelon Army units in both the MTO and ETO until the fighting stopped, as well as the British Army for the Italian campaign under Lend-Lease.

Some went to the US Marine Corps and lasted in service until early 1945 in divisional special weapon battalions. Due to the small number of Japanese tanks in the PTO, the Marine Corps' inventory of the 75mm GMC M3s were primarily employed as self-propelled artillery.

Combat in the Pacific

In August 1942, the Marine Corps' 75mm GMC M3s on Guadalcanal engaged Japanese tanks in a rare encounter. A description of that engagement appears in an article by Brigadier General H.T. Mayberry, Commandant of the Tank Destroyer School, for the December 1943 issue of *Military Review* magazine:

Twelve [current research indicates nine to ten] Japanese tanks led the assault across a sand-spit at the mouth of the river just at dusk. At a range of less than 100 yards, the self-propelled 75s destroyed ten of the tanks. The leading tank tried to maneuver and escape the devastating fire. It ran off the sand-spit and into the river, disappearing beneath the surface of the water. The last tank succeeded in crossing the spit but was destroyed while trying to make its escape down the beach.

Combat in North Africa

The only actual test of the 75mm GMC M3 as a tank destroyer occurred in North Africa on March 23, 1943 at a place known as El Guettar. A force of around fifty German tanks encountered the 601st Tank Destroyer Battalion, which was equipped with the 75mm GMC M3.

In the ensuing engagement, the 601st lost twenty of twenty-eight GMC M3s, and a supporting company lost seven fully-tracked tank destroyers. The tank destroyer crews claimed to have destroyed thirty German tanks and successfully repulsed the German attack. The Tank Destroyer Command celebrated the battle at El Guettar as confirmation of its doctrine.

Negative Opinions

Patton considered the action at El Guettar a costly failure due to the tank destroyers' high losses. He believed tank destroyers were only inferior tanks and that tanks could easily have fulfilled the tank destroyers' defensive anti-tank role and retained their offensive capabilities.

An important critic of the entire tank destroyer concept proved to be Lieutenant General Jacob L. Devers of the Armored Force, who stated in a letter to Lieutenant General McNair dated November 21, 1942:

> The separate tank destroyer arm is not a practical concept on the battlefield. Defensive anti-tank weapons are essentially artillery. Offensively, the weapon to beat a tank is a better tank. Sooner or later, the issue between ground forces is settled in an armored battle – tank against tank. The concept of tank destroyer groups and brigades attempting to overcome equal numbers of hostile tanks is faulty unless the tank destroyers are actually better tanks than those of the enemy.

About half of the Army's senior leadership came away with a very negative opinion of tank destroyers based on their use in North Africa. Major General John P. Lucas considered them unfit for service: 'I believe that the doctrine of an offensive weapon to slug it out with the tank is unsound.' Major General Ernest N. Harmon commented: 'Had more powerful guns been installed in tanks, tank destroyers would have been unnecessary.'

Numbers

Due to the introduction of fully-tracked tank destroyers, a large number of the surplus 75mm GMC M3/M3A1 – 1,360 examples – were converted into the Half-Track Personnel Carrier M3A1 configuration.

In early 1943, the Army's inventory of French 75s ran short, resulting in the 75mm Gun M3, as mounted in the M3 and M4 Medium Tank series, being grafted onto the M3 half-track as a substitute. However, at this point, the decision had already been made to concentrate on fully-tracked tank destroyers.

Wheeled GMC

Supplementing the 75mm GMC in tank destroyer companies was the 37mm GMC M6, consisting of a 37mm towed anti-tank gun modified to mount in the rear cargo bay of a 4 × 4 Dodge WC-55 Truck. The only armor on the vehicle was an armored shield for the vehicle's gun crew. Standardized in February 1942, a total of 5,380 examples came off the Chrysler Fargo Division's factory floor between April and October 1942.

Intended as a training vehicle, some found their way to North Africa in late 1942 or early 1943. They proved of limited usefulness during the subsequent fighting as the 37mm gun proved ineffective against German medium tanks. In some cases, the guns were removed and the trucks repurposed. Most were reverted to WC-52s; some of the 37mm guns were installed in Half-Track M3s.

Fully-Tracked GMC

To field a tank destroyer with a gun sufficiently lethal to deal with existing and anticipated German tanks, the Ordnance Department proposed mounting the 3in (76.2mm) M7 main gun from the M6 Heavy Tank into the open-topped chassis of the M3 Medium Tank. The project received authorization in October 1941, with the designation of the 3in GMC T24. The first example began testing in November 1941.

With the Japanese attack on Pearl Harbor the following month, the Army pushed the Ordnance Department to mount fifty First World War-era 3in anti-aircraft guns onto the open-topped chassis of M3 Medium Tanks in a semi-fixed, forward-firing position. Initially designated the 3in GMC T40, it was redesignated the 3in GMC M9. The design was of little value as the supply of weapons was small and aiming the weapon required moving the vehicle; a turreted solution was preferred and the T40 project came to a quick end.

What's Next?

Major General Gladeon M. Barnes had already decided that mounting a 3in (76.2mm) M7 Gun in a 360-degree rotating turret on the chassis of the newly-introduced M4 series of medium tanks looked like the best short-term option. Lieutenant General Andrew D. Bruce would have preferred waiting for the development of the ultimate tank destroyer. However, he was informed by McNair's AGF that he had to take what was offered.

The initial blueprints for this new tank destroyer configuration appeared in November 1941, with the vehicle designated the 3in GMC T35. A wooden mock-up appeared in January 1942. The diesel-engine-powered M4A2 Medium Tank was to be the base upon which an open-topped, rounded CHA turret armed with a 3in M7 Gun would sit.

The M4A2 chassis featured thinner hull armor than the standard tank model to save weight. The T35 would have no bow or coaxial .30 caliber machine guns for defense against infantry fitted, only a turret-mounted .50 caliber machine gun intended for anti-aircraft defense. This decision was regretted once the vehicle entered combat, as appears in the following passage from Headquarters Twelfth Army Group, *Immediate Report No. 58* dated September 21, 1944:

> Tank destroyers need a machine gun capable of firing on ground targets. The need to employ these weapons well forward requires that they be able to protect themselves against enemy infantry and snipers. The present anti-aircraft machine gun, because of its location and mount, cannot give this protection.

Based on information from US Army units fighting in the Philippines between December 1941 and April 1942 that sloped RHA armor plate had an advantage over vertical armor plates in deflecting projectiles, a decision came about that the T35 should feature both a sloped RHA upper hull and an RHA open-topped turret. The gun shield was of CHA construction.

The M10 Appears

Reflecting changes to its design, the second iteration of the T35 became the 3in GMC T35E1. It would go on to become the 3in GMC M10 in June 1942. Production began in September 1942 and continued until December 1943, with a total of 4,993 examples completed.

From a 1945 Army report titled *The General Board, US Forces, ETO, Report on Tank Destroyers* is this passage on the merits of basing the M10 on the chassis of the diesel-engine-powered M4A2 tank:

> The M10 motor carriage, powered by two diesel engines, proved to be a very good self-propelled gun mount. 1) The main advantages were the flexibility of the two motors, which made it possible to move after one had been knocked out or failed in operation; 2) The power of the diesel motors at low speed; 3) The increased range per gallon of fuel; and 4) The ease of motor maintenance of the diesel engines.

Lieutenant General Andrew D. Bruce thought highly of the M10's gun, but not the vehicle. The Armored Force questioned building it, as it didn't offer much in the way of enhanced capabilities other than a slightly larger gun compared to the existing first-generation M4A2 Medium Tank.

Into the Fray

The M10 in the Italian campaign acquired a solid reputation, as seen in a passage from the April 1944 Report of the New Weapon Board: 'This tank destroyer has become very popular with the using force, and they feel it is satisfactory except for its mechanical deficiencies [engines and suspension system], which are peculiar to vehicles on the medium tank chassis.'

In the US Army report titled *Lessons from the Italian Campaign* dated March 15, 1945 appears the following passage:

> The 3in gun of our M10 tank destroyer is the only comparable weapon at hand to the long-barreled German 75 and 88mm guns. Therefore, it is always desirable that tank destroyers overwatch the advance of our tanks. They are best placed in defilade positions as their armor is not as heavy [thick] as that of our medium tanks.

In a May 5, 1948 monograph from the Armored School titled *Armored Support of Infantry* is this passage describing a brief engagement during the July 1944 hedgerow fighting in Normandy, France involving Company A, 899th Tank Destroyer Battalion, which was equipped with the M10:

> As daylight approached, Company A, well aware that their 3in guns could not penetrate the heavy frontal armor of the Panther tanks,

maneuvered their tank destroyers to flanking positions where effective fire was placed on the enemy armor. One particular tank destroyer was forced to fire through a hedgerow at the invisible enemy. The platoon leader commanded the gunner to use APC-BDF [Armor-Piercing Capped, Base Detonating Fuze] and to start firing at the hedgerow 10 yards from a barn, traversing left about 80 yards and firing a round each 3 yards of that distance. The APC-BDF rounds penetrated the hedge without detonating, striking the enemy vehicles in the flank ... Three Panther, Mark V tanks were destroyed and one enemy half-track.

In *Immediate Report No. 58*, dated September 21, 1944, appears an extract on the M10's use in busting pillboxes on the German Westwall:

Usually about ten rounds neutralize a pillbox. On smaller types the last two or three will burst inside; on a larger one, of heavier construction, shutters will jam or the crew will surrender ... If the pillbox is attacked from the rear, the entrance is blown in, then one round of HE is fired into it and any occupants left immediately surrender.

We Need Overhead Protection

Like all the other self-propelled tank destroyers, lack of armor protection on the open-topped M10 could be a problem in certain tactical situations. In *Immediate Report No. 73* subtitled 'Combat Observations, Headquarters Twelfth Army' dated October 8, 1944 we see examples of that in the following extracts:

1. The M10 is extremely vulnerable to mortar and shell fragments entering the radiator. We have lost eight M10s in this way.
2. The M10 needs top armor protection for the crews against hand grenades and tree bursts. We installed 5/8-inch folding armor tops on our M10, which permits the crew commander to have all-around observation.

The lack of overhead armor protection for the M10 and other self-propelled tank destroyers and the problems it caused appears in a May 1950 research report prepared at the Armor School and titled *Employment of Four Tank Destroyer Battalions in the ETO*:

Several (TD veterans) wrote that TD self-propelled vehicles would have attained greater combat efficiency had they carried overhead as well as side armor. They also wrote that because it had not been provided, most units improvised their own. The improvisation ranged from a canvas spread, to deflect grenades, to metallic sheeting providing protection against overhead artillery bursts.

In one Army report, there is mention of tank destroyer men wanting to see observation slits installed in their turret sides so they would not have to expose themselves to snipers when looking out over the top of the turret walls. In some M10 Tank Destroyer battalions there appeared improvised periscopes.

A Very Different Environment

On the other side of the world, in the PTO, the M10 faced a host of unexpected issues impossible to resolve. Examples of this appear in extracts from an Armored School monograph dated May 1, 1948 titled *Armor in Jungle Operations*:

> The M10 tank destroyers were equipped with 16in tracks, and the old horizontal volute spring bogie-type suspension [VVSS]. Vines would become so tightly entangled in the bogie wheels that they would lock the wheel and cause it to slide on the track. In deep mud and over uneven terrain, tracks were easily thrown.

Another unforeseen problem was the heat and humidity of the jungle climate and the toll it took on the M10. In both New Guinea and the Philippines:

> Deterioration was by far the major difficulty encountered. Padding inside the tanks became mildewed and rotted and emitted such an offensive odor that it was necessary to remove it. Electrical cables, radios, voltage control regulators, periscopes, fire control instruments became so filled with fungus as to become unusable. Daily, this equipment was cleaned and dried in the sun; however, fungus still formed and ruined parts that were inaccessible to care ... Fire control instruments, when not in use, were left lying continuously in the sun during the daytime, and wrapped heavily in waterproof coverings during the night.

Tank Destroyer TO&E
Self-propelled tank destroyer battalions acted as tactical and administrative units and consisted of a headquarters and headquarters company, a reconnaissance company, three gun companies and a medical detachment. Each gun company had three platoons of four self-propelled guns each, totaling thirty-six guns in the battalion.

The Wrong Premise

The original doctrine for tank destroyers (be they towed or self-propelled) intended that they mass in large numbers behind the US Army's front lines. There, they would remain under their own command to await offensive operations by large German all-tank formations and strike a quick blow via a concentrated counterattack.

Unfortunately, as quickly discovered in North Africa and experienced for the rest of the war, German tanks tended to operate in combined arms teams that included infantry, artillery and anti-tank guns. This team concept was something the Tank Destroyer Command leadership had not foreseen and for which it proved unprepared in combat.

Less Aggressive

With the release by the Tank Destroyer Center of a revised tank destroyer manual dated July 18, 1944, it had finally adapted itself to reality. This was accomplished by removing the aggressive language used in the previous version, which caused many tank destroyer units in North Africa to go 'tank-hunting', thus increasing the number of casualties and loss of equipment. The original offensive spirit appeared in the tank destroyer's official motto: 'Seek, Strike and Destroy.'

An example of the tank-hunting issue appears in a report titled *Training Notes from Recent Fighting in Tunisia* dated May 15, 1943. The commander of the 899th Tank Destroyer Battalion stated:

> Tank destroyers must not be taught to go out to hunt tanks with the idea of getting behind them and hitting them. They must be taught to dig in, conceal themselves and wait for the tanks to come up. When this is done, the tank destroyers are easier to keep concealed, and there is less chance of giving the position away.

Major Issue

A major stumbling block for the Tank Destroyer Command/Center was that it was founded on the premise of acting primarily as a defensive force. Yet it formed part of an army that spent most of its time during the Second World War on the offensive.

Few field commanders had any awareness of how the tank destroyer doctrine worked. Nor would they allow their tank destroyer battalions to remain massed in the rear awaiting enemy tank attacks that might never occur. Instead, they parceled them out to infantry divisions, which lacked viable anti-tank weapons, depending on organic obsolete towed anti-tank guns (the 37mm and 57mm). Some tank destroyer battalions were attached to armored divisions.

The problem for many tank destroyer battalions was that their infantry counterparts considered them tanks and put them in the front lines where they proved extremely vulnerable. An example of this appears in a report by the 803rd Tank Destroyer Battalion dated July 6, 1944, fighting in the hedgerows of Normandy:

> In the earliest combat, there was a tendency on the part of the infantry commanders to order the destroyers out in front of the infantry. It cannot be emphasized enough that this is fatal. The destroyer cannot substitute for the tank inasmuch as it is lightly armored and no machine gun to keep hostile infantry down.

In a report by Colonel J.P. Barney, Jr, former commander of the 776th Tank Destroyer Battalion, addressed to men in training at the Tank Destroyer Center, he discussed the lessons he learned during the fighting in North Africa and warned about the misuse of tank destroyers as tanks:

> ... unit was directed to attack this armored unit [German], and did so with fire; the principal weapon of the destroyer, but actually closed in to the attack of the German armor. Its losses due to its lack of cover and armor were extremely heavy. This is brought out to show the effects of those same newspaper stories – Jack-the-Giant-Killer cannot work against a souped-up, long-barreled German 75 or an 88, and it is suicide for a [tank] destroyer to punch noses with a tank. The weapon of the destroyer is MASSED fire from the [Battalion] from the best concealed and prepared positions.

Secondary Roles

The new approved secondary roles identified in the July 1944 tank destroyer manual included some already in practice. They included the following:

a. Direct or indirect fire to reinforce or supplement that of artillery units.
b. Destruction of pillboxes and permanent defensive works.
c. Support of landing operations.
d. Defense of beaches against waterborne attack.
e. Roving gun and roving battery missions.

The downside of employing tank destroyers like the M10 in the artillery role appears in a passage from a September 1985 Army publication titled

Seek, Strike and Destroy: US Army Tank Destroyer Doctrine in World War II by Dr Christopher R. Gabel:

> Constant firing wore out the high-velocity tubes relatively quickly. Although tank destroyers maintained a basic load of anti-tank ammunition even when serving as artillery, the secondary mission, nonetheless, interfered with their ability to train for the anti-tank role. Some battalions split their companies between artillery and anti-tank missions to maintain a degree of anti-tank readiness. These drawbacks notwithstanding, battalion commanders agreed that morale improved when tank destroyers were employed in meaningful missions all the time, be they anti-tank or artillery.

M10s in Foreign Service

Of the 4,993 M10s constructed, 1,855 went to Lend-Lease, with the British Army receiving 1,648. The Red Army received 52, with another 155 going to the Free French Army. The Free French would go on to acquire around 100 more M10s from US Army stockpiles in the ETO.

The British Army assigned two slightly different designations to the M10s they received based on the turret counterweight configuration. They were, therefore, either the 3in Self-Propelled Mount (SPM) Mark I or the 3in SPM Mark II. An unofficial nickname for the vehicle, 'Achilles', does appear in some British Army wartime reports.

Not impressed with the tank-killing ability of the 3in Gun M7 on the M10, the British Army had 1,017 examples, mostly the 3in SPM Mark II, rearmed with the same 17-pounder gun that went into the Sherman Firefly. Those converted became known officially as the 'M10C' or the 'M10 17-pounder'. Besides the British Army, they also would see use with Commonwealth armies as well as the Free Polish Army.

Another M10 Iteration

McNair had initially planned on forming 200 tank destroyer battalions in 1942, which called for the building of around 11,500 tank destroyers. With that thought in mind, the Ordnance Department became concerned that there would not be a sufficient supply of M4A2 Medium Tank hulls.

As a back-up measure, they placed into production the M10A1, built on the modified chassis of the M4A3 gasoline-engine-powered medium tank. A total of 1,713 examples of the M10A1 came off the factory floor between October 1942 and December 1943. The majority remained in the United States as training vehicles. Others were reconfigured for other jobs, such as prime movers or armored recovery vehicles.

Lieutenant General McNair and the War Department became more realistic by October 1943 regarding the number of M10 series tank destroyer battalions required. That number finally dropped to just seventy-eight by 1944. The majority of the tank destroyer battalions served in the MTO and the ETO.

M18 Tank Destroyer

After several false starts, the Ordnance Committee, with input from the Tank Destroyer Center, approved the development and building of the gasoline-engine-powered 76mm GMC T70 on January 4, 1943. The first pilot vehicle appeared in April 1943.

By July 1943, another six pilots of the T70 were delivered for testing. The T70 embodied everything Lieutenant General Andrew D. Bruce wanted to see in the ultimate tank destroyer. The T70 would be the first American tank or armored fighting vehicle to feature an Ordnance Department-designed torsion bar suspension system.

After some (but not all) of its many design issues were resolved, production of the T70 began in great haste in June 1943, with the Tank Destroyer Command accepting the first batch the following month. The unresolved design problems soon came back to haunt the vehicle during service tests, resulting in constant modifications to the T70s as they came down the assembly lines.

In February 1944, the logistic and maintenance mess created by having so many vehicles with different types of modifications, based on when they came off the production lines, proved too much for all concerned. As a result, the majority of the T70s built up until that time (1,200 examples) went back to the factory. Once at the factory, they found themselves rebuilt to the same standard configuration.

The official standardization of the T70 as the 76mm GMC M18 took place in March 1944. The unofficial nickname assigned to the vehicle by the builder, Buick, was 'the Hellcat'. That name does not appear in any wartime US Army reports, but was approved for use by Major General Gladeon M. Barnes of the Ordnance Department in public releases in November 1944.

The 76mm Gun M1 series in the M18 was the same as mounted in some of the second-generation M4 series medium tanks, which would prove inadequate in the ETO at times. The M18 had both manual and powered hydraulic traverse systems. Not everybody proved as excited about the M18 as Lieutenant General Bruce of the Tank Destroyer Command/Center. From a report by the 813th Tank Destroyer Battalion in early 1945, 'the M10 is a superior TD to the M18 in every particular.'

Vehicle Numbers

The Ordnance Department and AGF envisioned building approximately 9,000 M18s, with 1,600 of those intended for Lend-Lease. That number was soon dramatically cut, as the AGF had then begun to favor towed tank destroyers. Besides, foreign armies showed little interest in the Hellcat.

Production of the M18 concluded in October 1944 with a total of 2,507 examples coming off the factory floor. As the desire for better-armed tank destroyers came to the forefront, the number of M18s required dropped. On June 26, 1944 the Ordnance Department approved taking 640 early-production M18s and converting them into what eventually became the Armored Utility Vehicle M39.

Good and Bad Features

The front, sides and rear of the M18's hull were only 0.5in (13mm) thick. The thickest armor on the M18 proved to be the front of its CHA gun shield at 1in (25mm). Ordnance Department testing of the M18 found that its armor could be penetrated by .30 caliber AP machine-gun ammunition at ranges up to 75 yards. The Tank Destroyer Center did not perceive the thin armor on the M18 as a disadvantage, as its superior mobility and speed were expected to offset that deficit.

From the Report of the New Weapon Board, dated April 27, 1944, are the first impressions made regarding the M18 in Italy, where they arrived in the spring of 1944:

> The tank destroyer and armored force personnel who examined this vehicle offered the observations that the armor is too thin and that the powertrain is too complicated ... There was no indication as to whether the increased speed would be a desirable characteristic, but the greater ease of control was very well-liked.

From Immediate Report No. 79 of the Twelfth Army Group dated October 1944 is an interesting observation of the usefulness of the M18's high-speed ability: 'The increased speed of the TD has proved to be a definite advantage in combat. Enemy gunners, apparently unable to estimate proper lead, consistently drop their shells to its rear.'

From an article in the *Field Artillery Journal*, July 1945 issue, titled 'Tank Destroyers at Work – Without the Book', is a passage on unusual employment of the M18 between February and March 1945 during the fighting for the Philippine capital of Manila:

> One section of M18 ... maintained near the river mouth in cover positions at all times. As lucrative targets appeared, the OPs [observation

posts] would notify the local 'fire department', and out would dash the destroyers to take up positions along the waterfront. Much good hunting was experienced in the form of tugs, barges and miscellaneous craft fleeing from the now trapped enemy positions [in Manila]. Small boats were strafed, tugs set afire and gasoline and ammunition barges blown sky-high … Much enemy personnel, material and supplies were thus prevented from being evacuated to Bataan and points north.

Up-Arming the M10 Series

On its own initiative, the Ordnance Department began considering the requirement for a superior anti-tank gun in early 1942 that could replace the existing 3in Gun M7. A prime candidate for this was the 90mm Anti-Aircraft M1, development of which had been approved in June 1938. The weapon was standardized in March 1940 with production beginning shortly after that.

Trials conducted of an M10 armed with a modified version of the 90mm Anti-Aircraft Gun M1 began in late 1942 and proved the concept generally viable. The experimental vehicle received the designation T71. The only serious design issue was the added weight of the larger gun. It aggravated the M10 series' already unbalanced turret design. The solution was the addition of turret-mounted counterweights.

Lieutenant General Bruce of the Tank Destroyer Command/Center disliked the T71, as he felt it was just another expedient tank destroyer to be forced on him, as was the M10. The AGF also did not seem to be that interested in the T71 but approved it as a development project only. In a February 9, 1943 letter from the AGF to the Ordnance Committee is the following passage: 'It is not desired by the Tank Destroyers [men] as a tank destroyer weapon since it is believed that the 3in gun [M7] has sufficient power. It is further felt that the Gun Motor Carriage, M10, is too heavy and too slow.'

Work Continued Anyway

The solution for a 90mm gun-armed M10 was to design a new turret. In March 1943, a wooden mock-up of a new turret received authorization. It was delivered in May 1943, followed by two soft steel examples in September 1943.

The testing of the T71 went well. Major General Gladeon M. Barnes of the Ordnance Department requested production of the vehicle in September 1943, but was snubbed by the Army Service Forces (ASF) because of the add-on request for two new medium tank projects, the T25 and T26.

By drumming up interest with the Armored Command and a new and more receptive commanding general at the Requirement Section of the AGF, Major General Barnes once again pushed for production of the T71 on October 4, 1943. His efforts proved successful, and production drawings for the vehicle were released in November 1943, followed by an order for 500 examples. At the same time, production of the M10 series was to cease.

The M36 Series Appears

Due to some T71 design issues that needed resolution, it took until February 1944 before the Tank Destroyer Board felt that the vehicle qualified for production. Rather than using the M10 chassis, a decision came about to mount the T71's new 90mm gun-armed turret on 500 yet-to-be-completed M10A1s, still on the factory assembly lines.

As events unfolded, there were just 300 available uncompleted M10A1s. These were converted to the T71 configuration between April and July 1944, after which the vehicle became standardized as the 90mm GMC M36. A dedicated tank gun version of the 90mm Anti-Aircraft Gun M1 became the 90mm Gun M3.

A Rare Bird

Erik Albertson, a volunteer at the WW2 Armor museum in Deltona, Florida, describes the background of an M36 in the collection:

The M36 we have is one of the direct-built M10A1s to M36s. We named it Balagan. Its M36 Serial Number is 117, with an M36 registration number of 40177445. There are no known M10A1 serial or registration numbers for our vehicle as it was one of the 300 turretless M10A1s built by Fisher Body Works after the M10A1 production. Balagan came off the production line in May 1944 when Fisher Body Works converted the interior of the hull for 90mm ammunition storage and installed the new turret and gun for the M36. Balagan is unique as it is one of eighty M36s in the world, one of only nine known surviving Fisher Body Works direct-build M36s and only one of three in the United States.

Send Us More

To create more M36s, 500 M10A1s employed for training duties were recalled to the factory for conversion to M36s between June and December 1944 to answer an urgent request for more M36s in the ETO. American industry converted another 413 examples between October and December 1944, but by December 20, 1944 there were just 236 examples in the ETO.

Having exhausted the stockpile of M10A1s, a total of 187 examples of the second-generation M4A3s, riding on the VVSS, had their existing 75mm gun-armed turrets removed and replaced by the 90mm gun-armed turrets of the M36. In this iteration, the vehicle became the M36B1.

An interesting comment on the M36 appears in Immediate Report No. 8, Headquarters ETO, dated December 11, 1944: 'All the men and officers questioned preferred to have a tank destroyer with the carriage and diesel engine of the M10, mounting the 90mm gun, for the following reasons':

a. The diesel engine has more power and steadier performance than the gasoline motor of the M36.

b. Danger of fire seemed greater, although in all cases where the M36 was hit, the motor was the last thing to burn, or the fire was confined entirely to the turret.

Anti-Tank Rounds

When the M36s appeared in the ETO in October 1944, their tank-killing rounds were the AP T33 Shot (APCBC-T) round, an improved version of the AP T77 Shot (AP-T) round, and the M82 (APCBC/HE-T) round.

As tests revealed that the M82 tended to shatter on contact with the Panther glacis, the T33 became the preferred choice. In a January 1945 report from the Office of the Chief of Ordnance is a description of the T33 round:

This is the most effective shot for the defeat of high obliquity caliber thickness homogeneous armor plate. The shot will defeat all plates of the German Pz. Kpfw. V Panther tank except the gun mantlet [gun shield]. It will penetrate the glacis plate of the Panther up to 1,100 yards range.

From the January 1945 report *United States vs. German Equipment* is a quote by the commanding general of the 2nd Armored Division. Regarding his impressions of the M36 series tank destroyers: 'Has not lived up to expectations, but when HVAP ammunition becomes available, it is hoped that it will be more effective.'

The HVAP ammunition referenced by the general began showing up in the ETO starting in March 1945. It received the designation HVAP T30E16 Shot. It also bore the label of an Armor-Piercing, Composite Rigid (APCR-T) round. From an Ordnance Department report is a description: 'A special hyper-velocity, armor-piercing round [HVAP] for attack of heavily armored vehicles … This shot will penetrate all plates of the German Pz. Kpfw. V Panther and King Tiger tanks.'

Notes on the M36

In Immediate Report (Combat Observations) No. 8, Headquarters ETO, dated December 11, 1944 appear comments regarding the M36 with the 702nd Tank Destroyer Battalion, which began receiving them in November 1944.

One extract mentions that the weight of the 90mm rounds, averaging around 40lb, made them hard to handle. Another excerpt indicates that the unit's M36s loaded up twelve to fifteen extra rounds in the turrets by removing them from their packing cases. The drivers stated that the gears were easier to shift than in the M10 and the vehicle easier to start.

Regarding engaging German tanks, the following passage appears in a December 29, 1944 report by the 776th Tank Destroyer Battalion in regards to an enemy attack they broke up, with the following results:

1. One Mark V hit through turret at a range of 1,300 yards – it did not burn.
2. One Mark V hit on left front at a range of 100 yards partially burned.

3. One Mark V hit above bogeys at a range of 1,900 yards did not burn.
4. One Mark V hit in driving sprocket at a range of 2,500 yards.
5. Three Mark IVs hit did not burn and were evacuated before being destroyed.
6. One half-track destroyed at a range of 2,700 yards burned completely.

Turret Traverse

The M10 did not have a power traverse system, as was the case with the M36. This disadvantage appears in an Army report dated September 28, 1944:

A power turret is needed to give speed in initial laying. The 628th and 813th Tank Destroyer Battalions have lost M10s to German tanks with power-operated turrets where it was a race for the initial shot between the hand traverse of the M10 and the power traverse of the German tank.

In the 2nd Armored Division report of March 1945, titled *United States vs. German Equipment*, Lieutenant Colonel John A. Beall, commander of the 702nd Tank Destroyer Battalion, answered a question regarding any possible advantage provided by the faster-powered turret traverse system of the M36:

a. Members of Company 'A' state that although the Mark V [Panther] has a much slower traverse than the M36, it had never been their experience that it was not sufficiently fast enough to track any of our tanks, other than the M4 traveling at a very high speed.
b. Company 'B', 702nd TD Battalion, has had no experiences where the speed of traverse actually affected the outcome of an encounter with a German tank. However, the added speed of traverse of the M36 is a definite advantage in coming onto the target.

Lieutenant Colonel Beall stated that it was the unanimous opinion of all men that the German tanks attempted to engage them at longer ranges whenever possible 'where their gun is able to penetrate our armor while the 90mm projectile is apt to ricochet from their armor'.

Aftermath

With the introduction in early 1945 of what became the M26 Heavy tank, armed with the same 90mm gun as the M36, a consensus arose among the Army's senior leadership that the tank destroyer concept had been seriously flawed from the beginning. By default, the tank destroyers had made a significant contribution to the fighting in the MTO and the ETO and took a heavy toll of enemy tanks, but their time had passed and on November 10, 1945 their independent command ceased to exist. To replace the tank destroyers, post-war Army infantry divisions would have organic tank battalions.

(**Below**) The 75mm Gun Motor Carriage (GMC) T12, seen here in August 1941, proved to be the US Army's first expedient tank destroyer. It consisted of the customarily towed 75mm Gun M1897A4 (including its upper carriage and gun shield), mounted on the modified chassis of the Half-Track Personnel Carrier M3, which had just entered service with the US Army in May 1941. (*TACOM*)

(**Opposite, above**) To provide the gun crew of the 75mm Gun Motor Carriage (GMC) T12 with an increased level of protection other than that provided by the small vertical gun shield that came with the 75mm Gun M1897A4, a small number of experimental gun shields appeared, such as the one pictured here. (*TACOM*)

(**Opposite, below**) In October 1941, an upgraded version of the 75mm Gun Motor Carriage (GMC) T12 became the 75mm Gun Motor Carriage (GMC) M3, with an example pictured here. Making room for the 75mm gun involved some design changes, including relocation of the vehicle's two 30-gallon fuel tanks to either side of the rear of the troop compartment. (*Patton Museum*)

(**Opposite, above**) The 75mm Gun Motor Carriage (GMC) M3 pictured here weighed 10 tons. Its thickest armor proved to be the armored windshield that protected both the driver and passenger, coming in at 13mm (0.5in). Frontal protection for the gun crew came from the 16mm (0.65in) gun shield, the sides and top of which were 6.5mm (0.25in). (*Pierre-Olivier Buan*)

(**Opposite, below**) Leveraging the design of the 75mm Gun Motor Carriage (GMC) M3, the Ordnance Department came up with the pilot vehicle pictured here: the 57mm Half-Track Gun Motor Carriage (GMC) T48. Armed with an American modified copy of a British 57mm anti-tank gun and protected by a newly-designed gun shield, it went only to Lend-Lease recipients. (*Dreamstime*)

(**Above**) In this picture, we see the breech end of the M1897A4 gun as mounted on a 75mm Gun Motor Carriage (GMC) M3. Also visible are the steel platform created to replace the lower carriage of the customarily towed weapon and the ammunition ready rack. Authorized main gun storage on the vehicle was fifty-nine rounds. Its rate of fire was six rounds per minute. (*Pierre-Olivier Buan*)

(**Above**) Starting in June 1941, the Ordnance Department tested many modified light-weight wheeled and tracked vehicles to study their suitability for mounting a 37mm anti-tank gun. As testing showed, the configuration was impractical. The next step involved the use of a larger 0.75-ton cargo truck. Standardized by the US Army in February 1942, it became the 37mm Gun Motor Carriage M6. An example is seen here in this dramatically-composed wartime photograph. (*Patton Museum*)

(**Opposite, above**) To come up with a suitable tank destroyer mounting a gun big enough to take on the best-protected enemy tanks, the Ordnance Committee approved mounting a 3in Anti-Aircraft Gun M1 in a fixed forward-firing position on the open-topped chassis of an M3 Medium Tank. In quick order, it became the 3in Gun Motor Carriage T-24, the T40 and finally the M9. The Tank Destroyer Board had no interest, and the program ended on August 20, 1942. (*TACOM*)

(**Opposite, below**) As consensus grew for mounting a 3in gun (the M7) in a fully-traversable turret, there appeared the 3in Gun Motor Carriage T35E1 pictured here, based on the modified chassis of a first-generation M4A2 Medium Tank. Combat reports had indicated the superiority of sloped armor, hence its appearance on the T35E1. (*Patton Museum*)

214

Weight empty: 51,605 lbs.
Weight loaded: 54,600 lbs.
Turning Diameter 68 ft.
Max. Height 8 ft. 7 in.
Height of bore above ground
zero elevation 7 ft. 8 in.

Maximum elevation of gun 15°
Maximum depression 2°
Maximum traverse right 16½°; left 16½°
Rounds of ammunition 40
Crew 6

(**Above**) Generally pleased with progress on development of the 3in Gun Motor Carriage T35E1, the Ordnance Committee recommended in June 1942 standardization of the vehicle as the 3in Gun Motor Carriage M10. However, before production commenced, a new five-sided, open-topped sloped RHA turret as seen here was designed. It was the turret that appeared on production M10s, which began coming off the factory floor in September 1942. (*Pierre-Olivier Buan*)

(**Opposite, above**) Pictured here is a preserved M10 Tank Destroyer in Free French Army markings. The M10 rolled off the factory floor with an RHA glacis of 38mm (1.5in) and a CHA gun shield with a maximum thickness of 55mm (2.25in). Visible on the vehicle pictured are welded-on studs for attaching factory-supplied add-on armor plates that, in the end, were never built. (*Public domain*)

(**Opposite, below**) The 13ft length and 1,990lb weight of the M7 3in gun, mounted in the M10 Tank Destroyer, was a continuing design issue as it badly unbalanced the vehicle's open-topped turret, especially on slopes. The eventual solution was the addition of two triangular counterweights totaling approximately 3,600lb, seen here fitted to the rear of an M10's turret. (*Patton Museum*)

The studs (auxiliary armor bosses) on the hull sides and turret of the M10 Tank Destroyer were eventually discontinued on the production lines, as seen on this museum vehicle. The only studs retained were on the M10's RHA glacis. To make up for the thin glacis armor, some M10 crews in the ETO added improvised protection, such as sandbags, on the glacis. *(Pierre-Olivier Buan)*

From the gunner's position on the M10 Tank Destroyer (note his manual turret traverse wheel) can be seen the vehicle's front hull compartment, with the driver on the left, the transmission in the center and the radio-operator on the right. The vehicle had no bow machine gun, although an earlier fully-tracked tank destroyer design under consideration had included one. *(Pierre-Olivier Buan)*

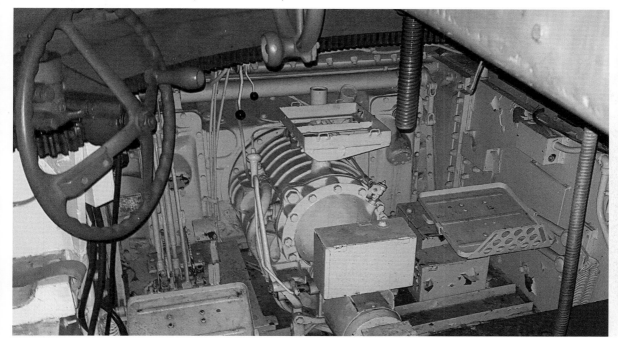

From the vehicle commander's position on the right-hand side of the M10 Tank Destroyer's turret, looking under the breech end of the 3in M7 Gun can be seen some of the upper hull (sponson) storage racks for the main gun ammunition on the vehicle's left side. In total, the M10 had authorized storage for fifty-four rounds of 3in ammunition. (*Pierre-Olivier Buan*)

Making all self-propelled tank destroyers open-topped was a way to keep their weight down, allowing for higher speeds and providing their crews with the best all-round visibility. Combat experience soon demonstrated that tank destroyer turret crews badly needed overhead protection. The result was that tank destroyer units came up with their own improvised armor arrangements as pictured here. (*Patton Museum*)

(**Opposite, above**) Besides using the diesel-engine-powered M4A2 Medium Tank chassis as the base for the M10 Tank Destroyer, the Ordnance Department decided to employ the gasoline-engine-powered M4A3 Medium Tank chassis for another version of the vehicle seen here, designated the M10A1. An external identifying feature is the visible lower rear hull engine exhaust screen, shared with the M4A3 Medium Tank. (*Patton Museum*)

(**Opposite, below**) The British Army thought little of the armor penetration abilities of the 3in guns fitted to the Lend-Lease M10 Tank Destroyers that they received. The decision came about to rearm them with the much more effective 17-pounder gun seen here. In this configuration, the vehicle was identified as the M10C or M10 17-pounder in British Army documents. (*Pierre-Olivier Buan*)

(**Above**) As the 17-pounder's barrel proved slimmer than that of the 3in Gun M7 fitted in the M10 Tank Destroyer, a gap was left in the gun shield (mantlet). British industry came up with a locally-designed small CHA housing that was welded onto the existing CHA gun shield as seen in this picture. A non-official wartime nickname for the 10C/M10 17-pounder was 'the Achilles'. (*Pierre-Olivier Buan*)

(**Above**) Lieutenant General Andrew D. Bruce, head of the Tank Destroyer Command, finally got what he considered his ideal tank destroyer when the first example of the 76mm Gun Motor Carriage (GMC) T70, later designated the M18, rolled off the assembly line in July 1943. The 20-ton vehicle rode on a torsion bar suspension system and had an unheard-of maximum level road speed of 60mph. (*Public domain*)

(**Opposite, above**) The builder of the 76mm GMC M18 pictured here, the Buick Motor Division of General Motors, named it 'the Hellcat'. The name did not appear in any wartime US Army documents. The M18 armament was the same 76mm gun fitted into second-generation M4 series tanks. The vehicle had authorized storage for forty-five main gun rounds. (*WW2 Armor Museum*)

(**Opposite, below**) Rather than using synchromesh transmission on all M4 series medium tanks that provided five speeds forward and one in reverse, the M18 Tank Destroyer had a newly-designed 900T Torqmatic (automatic three-speed) transmission. An example is seen in this picture of an M18's front hull compartment. Note the steering levers extend from the vehicle's front hull roof rather than the floor. (*WW2 Armor Museum*)

(**Above**) The M18 Tank Destroyer's air-cooled radial engine and the front hull-mounted transmission sat on rollers for ease of maintenance. The armored hull components that protected the engine and transmission also had rollers. When lowered, the rollers inside the armored hull components, such as the rear hull engine hatch pictured here, allowed for parts of the drivetrain to slide out for servicing or removal. (*WW2 Armor Museum*)

(**Opposite, above**) Early projections on the number of M18 Tank Destroyers to be built came in at around 9,000, of which more than 1,000 were expected to be delivered under Lend-Lease. In the end, only 2,507 examples of the vehicle rolled off the factory floor, with none going to Lend-Lease. Early-production examples exhibited some serious design issues due to the rush to place the vehicles into production. (*Richard and Barb Eshleman*)

The Ordnance Department possessed more foresight than the Army Ground Forces (AGF) and the Armored Force on the continuing trend of German tanks to feature ever-thicker armor and more powerful guns. Hence, Ordnance began considering mounting a modified 90mm anti-aircraft gun on an armored fully-tracked chassis in 1942. What eventually evolved proved to be the M36 Tank Destroyer pictured here, standardized in July 1944. (*WW2 Armor Museum*)

(**Opposite, above**) At first, the thinking was that an existing M10 Tank Destroyer turret could be successfully modified to accommodate a 90mm gun. That proved not to be the case, and a new CHA turret was designed. Unlike the M10's manually-traversed turret, the one on the M36 pictured here had a power traverse system. (*Pierre-Olivier Buan*)

(**Opposite, below**) Instead of having the new 90mm gun-armed turret go onto the M10 Tank Destroyer chassis, it went onto the M10A1 Tank Destroyer chassis, which in turn consisted of a thinly-armored chassis of the gasoline-engine-powered M4A3 Medium Tank. Both uncompleted M10A1s on the production lines and those returned from US Army Stateside training sites and Ordnance depots went through the transformation process. (*Richard and Barb Eshleman*)

(**Above**) As with the M10 Tank Destroyers, the crews of many M36 Tank Destroyers in the ETO quickly set about devising overhead armor protection arrangements, as is shown in this wartime image. German tankers rapidly learned that the M36 posed much more of a threat than any other American armored fighting vehicles. (*Patton Museum*)

(**Opposite, above**) Eventually, factory-designed overhead armor kits, as seen here, began appearing on late-production M36 Tank Destroyers. There was authorized storage for forty-seven rounds of main gun ammunition in the M36. A US Army manual states that the standard M82 AP round for the 90mm gun had a muzzle velocity of 2,670fps. (*Pierre-Olivier Buan*)

(**Opposite, below**) Due to the constant demand for more M36 Tank Destroyers in the ETO, American factories began to convert existing M10 Tank Destroyers into M36s. These vehicles received the designation M36B2. Another effort involved using the un-modified chassis of second-generation M4A3 (75) W tanks to mount the turret of the M36. Vehicles so modified became the M36B1, with an example pictured here. (*Pierre-Olivier Buan*)

(**Above**) On display at a US Army museum is an M36B1. A total of 187 examples came down the assembly lines. The .30 caliber bow machine gun proved a welcome addition to the vehicle's protection from enemy infantry. (*Chris Hughes*)

Chapter Six

Heavy Tanks

Upon the German invasion of Poland on September 1, 1939, the Ordnance Department began considering the requirement for a heavy tank. Until that time, the only heavy tank in the Army's inventory had been the approximately 43-ton First World War-era-designed Mark VIII, of which 100 came out of the factory doors between July 1919 and June 1920. All were pulled from service in 1932.

With the German invasion of the Netherlands and Belgium on May 10, 1940 and the French Army's failed intervention, the US Army Infantry Branch Chief recommended ten days later the development of a new heavy tank. It was to weigh anywhere between 50 and 80 tons. The Ordnance Committee recommended that the new heavy tank should not exceed 50 tons.

Pushing Along Development

The next month, oversight of tank development and doctrine passed from the Infantry Branch to the newly-formed Armored Command. Initial thinking regarding a new heavy tank revolved around a large multi-turreted vehicle armed with a variety of cannons and machine guns. Approval of the idea took place on July 11, 1940, with the proposed vehicle designated the Heavy Tank T1.

A more realistic appraisal of the T1 design appeared in October 1940, when the idea of a multi-turreted vehicle was replaced by the concept of a single-turreted tank. The turret was to be armed with a modified version of the 3in (76.2mm) T9 anti-aircraft gun. Instead of a coaxial machine gun, the design called for the 37mm Gun M5E1.

Due to the rush to field the new heavy tank, a contract went out in August 1940 for two pilots, the T1E1 and the T1E2. Both had air-cooled, radial engines; the difference was the drivetrain. The T1E1 had a gasoline-electric drive system that did not call for a transmission. The T1E2 and a follow-on T1E3 pilot used torque converters in place of transmissions.

A standard synchromesh transmission as used in the M3 and M4 Medium Tank had been considered for the T1 series but was rejected as not sufficiently robust to handle the tank's weight. It would also have required a new heavy-duty clutch, but none were then available.

Eventually the T1E2, with a CHA turret and upper hull, became the M6. The T1E3, with a welded RHA turret and CHA upper hull, was designated the M6A1. The two tanks each had an approximate weight of 63 tons. The tanks' gun shields had a maximum armor thickness of 102mm (4in) and the glacis 83mm (3.25in).

A description of a torque converter appears in a passage from a War Department manual, *Heavy Tank M6 and M6A1*, dated February 5, 1943:

> A flexible coupling connects the engine to the torque converter, no propeller shaft being used on this vehicle. The hydraulic torque converter is a form of hydraulic transmission which applies the engine horsepower to the final drive ... Fluid, such as No. 1 Diesel fuel, is the operating medium of the torque converter, there being no mechanical connection between the input and output ends of the torque converter. Since the drive is through fluid, no clutch is used on the vehicle. A pedal, placed in the position usually occupied by a clutch pedal, serves as a transmission brake pedal. In order to shift, the converter turbine and transmission gears must be slowed down or stopped by means of the brake. Two forward speeds and one reverse speed are provided.

Numbers

Between German military successes on the battlefield and the Japanese attack on Pearl Harbor, the United States found itself in a fearful place in 1940/41. The country's civilian and military leadership reacted as best they could with limited information on the enemy's capabilities and intentions.

Despite design flaws, more than 1,000 M6/M6A1 tanks were authorized for production, with the first M6 appearing in December 1942. A single production example of the M6A1 also came down the assembly line around the same time.

The large number of unproven M6 series tanks ordered came from President Franklin D. Roosevelt's unrealistic call in January 1942 for 500 heavy tanks in 1942 and 5,000 more in 1943. Interestingly, by August 10, 1942 the US Army's Services Forces (ASF) had decided it did not want the M6; it only wanted 115 examples of the T1E1 pilot configuration for US Army testing and all the M6/M6A1s allocated for Lend-Lease.

Even as production of the M6/M6A1 began, opinions on the need for a heavy tank had turned. On December 7, 1942 Lieutenant General Devers, commander of the Armored Force, wrote to Lieutenant General McNair, stating: 'Due to its tremendous weight and limited tactical use, there is no requirement in the Armored Force for the heavy tank. The increase in the power of the armament of the heavy tank does not compensate for the heavier armor.'

So appeared the death warrant for the heavy tank M6 series. In the end, only forty-three were manufactured, including pilots, although in August 1944 the Ordnance Corps suggested arming fifteen examples of the T1E1 with the 105mm Gun T5E1 for attacking fortifications. Army Ground Forces (AGF) had little interest in the proposal. Eventually, the matter showed up on the desk of General Dwight D. Eisenhower, Supreme Commander of the Allied Expeditionary Forces in Europe (SHAEF). He considered the concept impractical and rejected the vehicles, by then designated the M6A2E1.

Another Path for a Heavy Tank

The only Army heavy tank to reach front-line service during the Second World War proved to be the M26. Its beginnings go back to early 1942 when some within the Ordnance Department began to consider an eventual replacement for the M4 series of medium tanks. Rather than having upper and lower hulls as with the existing medium tank, the proposed replacement was to have only a lower hull under the concept referred to as 'space engineering'.

By doing away with the upper hull, a great deal more armor could go onto the lower hull, with the hopeful intention of maintaining the same weight as the existing medium tank and lowering the center of gravity. Armament was to be the then-in-development 76mm Gun M1. Power would be a version of the Ford GAA gasoline-powered-engine that went into the M4A3 Medium Tank.

Getting There

Many experimental vehicles built in varying numbers began appearing in January 1943. All were platforms to test various design features and components and their suitability for inclusion in a final product. These would include the T20 through the T25 Medium Tank series.

The T23 proved a novel design as the Ordnance Department fitted it with an electric drive system. However, testing of the T23 showed it to be unsuitable for combat due to its maintenance requirements. Despite that, 250 came off the assembly lines with most going directly into storage. The main gun on the T23 was the 76mm Gun M1.

With the advent of the T25 series, the main gun became the 90mm Gun M3, the same weapon arming the M36 Tank Destroyer. The heaviest fixed round it fired topped out at about 44lb.

A limited production run of fifty vehicles received authorization, with forty of those the T25 Medium Tank and ten of the T26 Medium Tanks. Major General Thomas J. Hayes Jr of the Ordnance Department wanted 500 examples of each built, but that request went nowhere.

Design studies on the yet-to-be-built T25 and T26 estimated that the T25 would weigh about 40.5 tons and the T26, with thicker armor, around 47.5 tons. These were much heavier than initially planned as some of the extra weight on the tanks could be attributed to the roughly 2-ton electric drive system. The Armored Board decided at the last minute to have the new Detroit Transmission Torqmatic automatic transmission installed in the T25 and T26 in place of an electric drive system.

From a Detroit Transmission 1944 sales brochure is a passage touting the Torqmatic transmission's advantages:

> The increased vehicle performance obtained with Torqmatic transmission clearly demonstrates that the unit is a highly efficient means of transmitting power to the tracks or wheels of a vehicle. The cushioning effect and the automatic features of the Torque Converter that simplify driving and reduce physical effort with the ability to shift, when necessary, from one range to another under full torque have marked this type of transmission as a unit which can be adapted to many types of heavy-duty vehicles.

A New Drive System for Tanks

A tracked vehicle with an electric (hybrid) drive system relies on a gasoline/diesel engine that powers an electric generator. The generator's output drives two electric traction motors, each attached to one of the vehicle's two drive sprockets, each engaging the vehicle's tracks. (Two engines and generators can be used to provide greater capacity and redundancy.)

The design eliminates the traditional mechanical transmission/differential and any driveline between the engine and drive sprockets. Mechanical transmissions are complex and require sophisticated manufacturing capacity, increasing in all respects for larger, heavier tanks.

The potential savings with an electric (hybrid) drive system include cost, weight, maintenance and power loss to the drive sprockets during gear changes, as well as possibly less demand for interior space. Steering can be controlled electrically instead of mechanically (by differential speed or braking by the drive motors), possibly reducing wear and tear and maintenance.

Reflecting the incorporation of the Torqmatic automatic transmission, the T25 and T26 became the T25E1 and T26E1. The only exceptions in the switch to the automatic transmissions were two T25s and a single T26 which were built with an electric drive system. The reason was to compare test results from both drivetrain designs.

Finalizing a Candidate

Delivery of the forty T25E1s and the ten T26E1s took place between February and May 1944. Maximum armor thickness on the T25E1 was 89mm (3.5in) on the gun shield and the glacis was 75mm (3in). For the T26T1, the gun shield topped out at 114mm (4.5in) and the glacis at 107mm (4.25in).

Testing the vehicles continued through the summer of 1944. In June 1944, likely to convince tankers in thin-skinned M4s that help was on the way, the Ordnance Department ordered that all the various versions of the T26 Medium Tank series bear the label Heavy Tanks.

Testing indicated the need for some design changes on both vehicles, one of which was main gun ammunition storage. As delivered, the T26E1 had authorization for only forty main gun rounds, far less than combat experience suggested necessary.

In the ETO, those concerned with tanks demanded room for seventy main gun rounds in the T26E1, a design feature solved by rearranging fighting compartment components and doing away with the vehicles' wet ammunition storage configuration. In comparison, the Panther had authorized storage for eighty-two main gun rounds.

Both the T25E1 and T26E1 rode on a torsion bar suspension system that had first appeared on the T23E3. Before that point, the T23 Medium Tank rode on an HVSS system, as had the T25 Medium Tank.

The T25E1's 19in-wide tracks did not provide sufficient flotation, causing the vehicle to dig in to surfaces unacceptably. The recommendation was to install the 24in-wide track system of the T26E1 on the T25E1. However, at this point, reports from the ETO emphasized the need for better-armed and armored tanks able to slug it out with the Panther. The Armored Board interest, therefore, switched to the more heavily-armored T26E1, sidelining the T25E1 from further consideration.

The T26 series

The Armored Board's side-by-side testing of the single T26 with electric drive against the T26E1 and an improved model (with the new automatic transmission) designated the T26E3 began in November 1944. These tests helped identify advantages and disadvantages of the different vehicles.

Due to concerns regarding the electric drive's complexity and the belief that the typical tank mechanic would be unable to service it, the T26 was dropped from further consideration. With that action, the Armored Board now focused on the T26E3.

A Debate

The continued development of the T26 series initiated a great deal of discussion among Major General Gladeon M. Barnes of the Ordnance Department, McNair of the AGF and Devers, who had become Commander European Theater of Operations, US Army (ETOUSA) in May 1943. Many others of all ranks were also involved in the discussions.

In a memo dated November 7, 1943 from Brigadier General Joseph M. Colby of the Ordnance Department to Major General John K. Christmas (also of the Ordnance Department), Colby recommended immediate production of the T26 with its electric drive system:

> I recommend production of this vehicle at once, using the electric drive. The Medium Tank, T26E1, which is basically the same tank except that it has the torsion bar suspension and Torqmatic transmission, can be made into a good tank. However, from the standpoint of efficiency and operation, I feel that the electric drive is definitely superior.

Pushing for the T26E3 tank, on November 13, 1943 Devers requested that the War Department authorize 250 examples of the tank as quickly as possible. He backed up his request by stating that the British War Office had decided to ask for 500 of the T26E3s under Lend-Lease.

McNair, always a strong proponent of the doctrinally-corrupt tank destroyers, had a few weeks later written to General George S. Marshall, the Army's Chief of Staff, a rebuttal of Devers' request:

> There can be no basis for the T26 [T26E3] tank other than the conception of a tank-versus-tank duel – which is believed unsound and unnecessary ... There has been no indication that the 76mm anti-tank gun is inadequate against the Mark VI [Tiger] ... Tank destroyers of either 76mm or 90mm caliber thus can support an armored division or other unit in whatever degree is necessary to protect them against hostile tanks, leaving the friendly tanks themselves free for their proper mission [exploitation].

In a December 9, 1943 letter by Barnes to McNair endorsing Devers' request for 250 T26E3 tanks, he stated that both the T25 and T26 should go into production to '... have available tanks of greater firepower and greater armor protection, should they be required'. He also recommended an immediate order for 500 of the T23, with the electric drive system, which did not happen. Also, 500 each of the T25 and T26 were requested for use during the Italian campaign. The reason was German employment of Tiger I tanks in that theater with its thick frontal armor and the restrictive, maneuvering-channeling Italian terrain.

As Marshall tended to support the decisions of his overseas commanders, it seemed that the production of the T26E3 had now received the support it needed to overcome McNair's objections. On December 25, 1943 Marshall informed Devers that his request for the 250 T26E3 tanks had been approved, but also mentioned that it might take as long as nine months before production could begin due to production bottlenecks.

Change in Command

Another issue regarding the T26E3 came to the forefront when Devers left his post as Commander ETOUSA in January 1944. His replacement, Eisenhower, had objected to the T26E3 in November 1943, and there remained some question regarding his current views on the subject. The Joint Chiefs of Staff sent Marshall a recommendation on January 21, 1944 suggesting that any decision on the T26E3 program's fate wait until Eisenhower had reviewed the matter.

Marshall, in the meantime, assigned Lieutenant General Thomas T. Handy, an officer on his staff, to review the issue and make a recommendation. Handy stated in his report: 'The Germans are making and using heavy tanks. It is another case of having to go ahead without waiting for long field tests. We may make a mistake and be blamed for it. That it is far better than not having a weapon that is needed.'

With that, Marshall decided that the T26E3 was a necessary weapon for the ETO. He cabled Eisenhower on January 15, 1944 to ask him if he had any objections to shipping the tank to Western Europe. Eisenhower replied that he did not.

Too Little, Too Late

Production of the five-man T26E3 began in November 1944 and continued through to the end of 1945, with 2,212 examples eventually completed. The roughly 46-ton vehicle had a maximum speed on level roads of 25mph, and for short periods it could attain 30mph, also on a level road. The tank's glacis was 100mm (4in) and the turret gun shield 114mm (4.5in). The sides and rear of the turret came in at 75mm (3in). It had authorized storage for seventy main gun rounds.

The massive surprise attack that began the December, 1944 Battle of the Bulge added tremendous urgency to the T26E3 program. Six days later, orders were cut to ship twenty T26E3s to the ETO as quickly as possible. The other twenty, in the meantime, were retained by the Armored Board for further testing.

The first twenty T26E3s arrived on the European continent in January 1945. The tanks all went to the 12th Army Group, which in turn assigned them to the First Army. In quick order, the First Army split them between two of its armored divisions: the 3rd Armored and 9th Armored.

To assist with the introduction and evaluation of these new tanks (and other weapons) in the ETO, Major General Barnes of the Ordnance Department led a group of Army specialists and civilians referred to as 'the Zebra Mission'. The Zebra Mission was responsible for training Army tankers to effectively operate and maintain the new tank, especially its 90mm main gun.

The 2nd Armored Division Impressions

In the March 1945, 2nd Armored Division report titled *United States vs. German Equipment* there is a quote by Captain John A. McNary: 'Little is known about the M26 tank, but from observation of the 90mm gun on the tank destroyer [M36], the men still feel that the high-velocity 75mm and 88mm that the Germans use is more effective against armor. Our guns still lack velocity.'

In the same report appears another passage on the view American tankers had of the yet-to-be-delivered M26: 'None of us have ever seen a T26. But from what we understand, it is certainly a step in the right direction. It sounds like it gives us a gun and armor that can at least begin to compare with what we are fighting against.'

A Name is Assigned

In March 1945, the T26E3 was officially standardized as the M26. According to the US Army's official history of the Second World War, in the volume titled *The Ordnance Department: On Beachhead and Battlefront*, the M26 received the official nickname 'General Pershing' at the same time.

On May 7, 1945, when the war ended in the ETO, 310 examples of the Pershing were on hand. However, only the first twenty saw combat against German late-war tanks and self-propelled guns.

Meeting the Enemy

Reflecting the late stage of the war in the ETO and the continued degradation of the German military forces' capabilities, encounters between German tanks and self-propelled guns and the Pershing proved infrequent, and when they did occur, only involved a couple of vehicles.

Comparing Performance of the Pershing and Panther

When comparing the Pershing to the Panther, its closest wartime competitor, we see some interesting differences. The Pershing comes in at 46 tons; the Panther at 50 tons. Both tanks rode on a torsion bar suspension system; the Pershing's ground pressure was 12.5psi, the same as the Panther's. Ground pressure is the ratio of a tank's weight to the surface area supporting it; i.e. so many pounds per square inch. At that time, ground pressure was typically referred to as flotation. The term does not mean the vehicle's capability to float in water, but instead its ability to travel over soft ground. High ground pressure relative to an opponent's means more restricted maneuver and especially advance, possible limitations on cover and concealment, likely higher fuel consumption, etc.

The Pershing's gasoline engine produced 500 gross hp at 2,600rpm. In comparison, the Panther's gasoline engine produced 690 gross hp at 3,000rpm. The Pershing's speed on level roads was 25mph; the Panther's 28mph. The gross power-to-weight ratio on the Pershing was 10.8hp/ton, while on the Panther it was 13.8hp/ton.

Noted tank historian and author, the late Richard Hunnicutt, in his groundbreaking book on the Pershing tank, compared it to the German Panther and Tiger I tank. He decided that 'based on the criteria of firepower, mobility and protection, the Panther would have to be rated first followed by the Pershing and lastly the Tiger I.'

The first combat engagement between a Pershing and an enemy tank took place on the evening of February 26, 1945. From a wartime report, the encounter is described by the tank commander and two other tank crews:

The T26E3 tank was pulled up against the roadblock to watch for enemy movement; a fire directly in back of the tank and to one side silhouetted the turret, which was all that was showing over the roadblock. A German Tiger tank [Tiger I] just around the corner of a building about 100 yards away fired three shots at the tank. The first shot entered the turret through the coaxial [machine-gun] mount, killing the gunner and loader. A second shot hit the muzzle brake and the end of the gun tube, jarring off the shot, which was in the chamber. This discharge of the shell caused the gun tube to swell about halfway down, even though the projectile went out of the tube. A third shot glanced off the upper right-hand side of the turret, striking the [tank commander's] cupola hatch cover, which was left open. The Tiger backed up on a pile of debris and was abandoned.

The loader of the tank was later captured and admitted that his tank had done the firing and had been abandoned.

The T26E3 tank was evacuated, repaired and recommitted for combat on 7 March 1945. A new barrel came from an M36 Tank Destroyer.

On March 6, 1945 leading elements of the 3rd Armored Division entered the German city of Cologne. Corporal Clarence Smoyer, a gunner on a Pershing, recalled his vehicle's encounter with an enemy tank that day in an interview conducted by volunteers of the former Patton Museum of Armor and Cavalry:

> Eventually, a German tank [Panther] came around the side of a building; by the time we got an armor-piercing shell into the cannon, he realized that there were a bunch of us over there and he backed up. We fired armor-piercing shells through the building that he backed up behind, thinking we might get a lucky hit and knock him out, which we didn't ...
>
> When the lead tank was hit, they radioed us to go down another street, to take out the German tank. Somehow or another, the German tank crew knew what we were doing; they came up to the intersection we were approaching and were waiting for us. Our plan had been to come up to the intersection corner and slowly pull around just far enough to see where the German tank was, and then let me turn the turret and get a shot off. After that, we would quickly back up.
>
> As soon as our driver saw the gun on the German tank, less than 100 yards away, instead of stopping the tank to give me a chance at a shot, he floored the throttle as fast as he could through the intersection, and I fired on the move and hit him [the Panther] right before the gun shield. Because we weren't sure if we killed everybody in the tank, we fired two more shots into it, and that was the end of the German tank and crew.

Send Us More

On March 8, 1945 Major General Gladeon M. Barnes of the Ordnance Department visited Eisenhower's headquarters, showing him pictures of the T26E3. The same day, Eisenhower cabled General Brehon B. Somervell, the commander of the Army Service Forces (ASF), requesting the immediate shipment of any available T26 tanks:

> Combat operations to date, while limited, convince me that the T26 tank has what it takes. Barnes thinks you may have some 200

available for shipment now. Urge strongly that you get every tank of this type to us as quick as possible, displacing M4s or other types as necessary to find requisite tonnage. Would appreciate immediate advice as to what you can do so we can arrange assignment and get maximum number into current action at earliest possible date.

Going to the Pacific

With the end of combat operations in the ETO, thoughts turned to sending the Pershing tanks to the PTO as an experiment. Heavy losses of M4 series tanks to Japanese anti-tank defenses had become a growing concern during the fighting for Okinawa (May till June 1945). The better-armed and armored Pershing could be the answer, as believed by some.

As appears in a memo dated May 25, 1945, others thought the tank's size and weight would be a problem on Okinawa's rough terrain: 'Suitability of M26 heavy tank is questionable because of its weight and width. Terrain features and restricted communications nets ... as well as difficulties in handling shipment and over-land movement must be considered.'

The twelve Pershing tanks shipped to the PTO arrived on July 21, 1945, too late to see combat on Okinawa. They remained on the island for possible employment during the planned invasion of Japan, but with that country's surrender on August 15, 1945, they were no longer required.

Other Versions

Before the introduction of the Pershing into the ETO, plans called for a modified version, armed with a 105mm howitzer. It received the designation M26E2, with delivery of a pilot slated for April 1945. Early thinking revolved around having more of the T26E2s manufactured than the M26. However, combat experience in the ETO led to the demand for only the M26s, armed with the 90mm main gun.

In the end, only 185 examples of the T26E2 appeared by the end of 1945. None would see combat in the Second World War. Post-war, the howitzer-armed tank received the designation M45, with some seeing service during the Korean War (1950–53).

Based on the M4A3E2 assault tank's success in the ETO, the Ordnance Department began to consider development of an up-armored version of the Pershing in February 1945. The proposed vehicle received the designation T26E5, with production starting in June 1945. The surrender of Japan resulted in program cancelation after only twenty-seven examples came down the assembly line.

A Bigger Gun

Awareness of the German Tiger II, which the British Army in France first encountered in July 1944, prompted the Ordnance Department to design a more potent 90mm main gun than the existing 90mm Gun M3. The intention was to have a 90mm gun that could match the range and penetration capabilities of the 8.8cm (88mm) KwK 43 Gun mounted in the Tiger II.

As a test, a version of the T15 gun that went into a T26E1 tank received the designation T15E1. Whereas the 90mm Gun M3 had a barrel length of almost 17ft, the 90mm Gun T15E1 came in at around 23ft.

Because of the increased length of the cartridge case for the 90mm Gun T15E1, the T25E1 turret (the same as on the M26) proved too cramped, thereby forcing the use of two-piece main gun rounds. When modified to accept the two-piece rounds, the gun became the 90mm gun T15E2.

In March 1945, the Ordnance Department authorized production of 1,000 examples of the T26E1 tank, armed with the T15E2 gun. In this configuration, the future production examples were to be assigned the designation T26E4 and built in lieu of an equal number of Pershing tanks. For test purposes, a T26E1 armed with a T15E2 gun, firing the separated main gun rounds, stayed in the United States.

The Big League

A T26E1 pilot tank fitted with the T15E1 main gun and firing the original one-piece rounds went off to the ETO, arriving at a 3rd Armored Division maintenance battalion on March 15, 1945. Apparently, it acquired the unofficial nickname of the 'Super Pershing' at that time.

Everybody's goal in March 1945 seemed to revolve around pushing the so-called 'Super Pershing' into front-line service where it could hopefully engage in battle with a Tiger II. To even the odds of a one-on-one encounter with a Tiger II, the personnel of the 3rd Armored Division's maintenance battalion welded armor cut from the glacis of a knocked-out Panther tank onto their Super Pershing's gun shield section. Also, they attached additional armor to the tank's glacis.

On two occasions, the Super Pershing engaged German armored fighting vehicles, coming out the victor twice, but neither has been confirmed as a Tiger II. The Super Pershing went off to the scrappers after the war.

A Monster Tank

Beside the M26 Heavy Tank, relabeled as a medium tank in the immediate post-war period, the Ordnance Department also pursued other heavy tank programs. One of these proved to be the massive, almost 95-ton Heavy

Tank T28, armed with a newly-developed 105mm gun designated the T5E1. The heaviest separated round for the gun weighed in at 74lb.

The T28 came with two sets of tracks on either side of the hull. The two sets aided in distributing the vehicle's massive weight and thus lowering ground pressure. The outer sets of tracks and the 101mm-thick (4in) armored skirt armor were removable and could be towed behind the vehicle when operating on hard surfaces; maximum speed on level roads was only 8mph.

The Ordnance Department envisioned the T28 used in taking on the defensive fortifications of the Westwall, which guarded the western German border. Armor protection on the T28 came in at 292mm (11.5in) on the gun shield, with the front of the turretless hull 305mm (12in) thick.

Initially, the Ordnance Department saw a need for twenty-five examples of the T28, but that number kept dropping as the AGF saw no requirement for the vehicle. In March 1945, reflecting the fact that the vehicle had no turret, it received the new label of the 105mm Gun Motor Carriage (GMC) T95. The two pilots of the vehicle did not appear until after the Second World War.

Too Late

To answer the threat posed by German late-war tanks, a recommendation from the Ordnance Committee called for the development and construction of four related heavy tank pilots. Two received the designation of the T29 and featured the 105mm Gun T5E1. The other two, armed with the 155mm Gun T7, became the T30. Modifications to the T29 and T30 pilots would result in sub-variants for both tanks.

In May 1945, the Ordnance Department approved rearming the two T30 pilots with a modified anti-aircraft gun designated the 120mm Gun T53. The gun offered better armor penetration capabilities than the 105mm gun in the T29 or the 155mm gun in the T30. When fitted with the 120mm gun, the two rearmed T30s found themselves redesignated the T34.

The weight of the various iterations of the pilot heavy tanks came in at approximately 71 tons. Their gun shields had a maximum thickness of 279mm (11in) and their glacis 102mm (4in).

There were also four pilots authorized in February 1945 for a heavy tank designated the T32, armed with the 90mm Gun T15E2. It weighed about 60 tons and had a maximum armor thickness of 298mm (11.75in) with 127mm (5in) on its glacis.

Neither the T32 nor any other late-war heavy tank designs appeared until after the Second World War. In the immediate post-war period, they became experimental test beds before they were pulled from service.

(**Opposite, above**) With the successful German invasions of Poland in September 1939 and France in the summer of 1940, the Ordnance Department began considering a heavy tank, seconded by the Infantry Branch Chief. At that time, the US Army regarded any tank weighing over 30 tons as a Heavy Tank. After considering a multi-turreted tank, the US Army eventually settled on the single-turreted design seen here labeled the Heavy Tank T1E2. (*Patton Museum*)

(**Above**) Another view of the approximately 55-ton pilot Heavy Tank T1E2, with a CHA turret and hull. Main armament was the 3in (76.2mm) T7 Gun, with a coaxial 37mm gun. The Heavy Tank shared some design features with the M3 series of medium tanks, including the CHA vehicle commander's cupola. Note the rear-facing, turret-mounted .50 caliber machine-gun mount. (*Patton Museum*)

(**Opposite, below**) Continued refinement of the pilot Heavy Tank T1E2 eventually resulted in construction of what became the 63-ton Heavy Tank M6 pictured here. A version with an RHA hull received the designation of the M6A1. The Armored Force saw no requirement for a Heavy Tank at that time, and the program came to an end in December 1940. (*TACOM*)

With the demise of the M6 series of heavy tanks, the Ordnance Department turned its interest to up-gunned versions of the never-fielded Medium Tank T20 series. The weapon of choice was the 90mm Gun M3. With that gun, there appeared the T25 and T26 Medium Tanks. In September 1944, the T25 program ended, followed by the T26, replaced with an improved version seen here, the T26E1. (*Patton Museum*)

As development continued with the T26E1, of which ten were built, its design eventually evolved into the Medium Tank T26E3. It had authorized storage for seventy main gun rounds, with the eight unprotected rounds seen here in the vehicle's turret. These were considered the ready rounds, with the remaining sixty-two main gun rounds stored horizontally under the turret floor in a wet stowage arrangement. (*Patton Museum*)

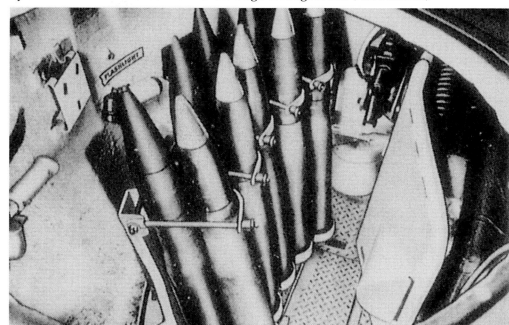

The five-man Medium Tank T26E3 pictured here weighed around 46 tons and had a height of almost 12ft. By comparison, the standard second-generation M4 Medium Tank series armed with the 76mm gun had a height of almost 10ft. The glacis on the T26E3 had a thickness of 102mm (4in), and the turret gun shield 114mm (4.5in). *(TACOM)*

On June 29, 1944 the T26E3 was designated a Heavy Tank for morale purposes. Production began in November 1944, with the vehicle receiving its official designation of the Heavy Tank M26 in March 1945. It also acquired its official nickname of 'the General Pershing'. *(TACOM)*

(**Opposite, above**) The Pershing seen here received power from a slightly different version of the 500hp gasoline-powered, liquid-cooled, GAA engine used in the M4A3 Medium Tank and its variants. It also shared the same controlled heavy-duty truck-type differential system. (*Pierre-Olivier Buan*)

(**Above**) In this view of the rear of a Pershing tank, the engine exhaust muffler is visible. The vehicle's powerpack, consisting of the engine, transmission and controlled differential, could be removed from the vehicle as a single assembly. Rather than the single bottom hull escape hatch, the Pershing had two: one for the driver and the second for the assistant driver/bow gunner. (*TACOM*)

(**Opposite, below**) The first twenty examples of the Pershing did not arrive in the ETO until January 1945, with ten going to each of the 3rd and 9th Armored Divisions. The first combat engagement between the new American tank and a German Tiger I tank took place on February 26, 1945 with the enemy tank prevailing. (*Patton Museum*)

Pictured in a post-war scrapyard somewhere in Europe is a single example of the pilot Heavy Tank T26E4, with its turret reversed rearward, armed with a new, more powerful and longer-barreled 90mm gun designated the T15E1. The tank, nicknamed 'the Super Pershing', had been rushed to the ETO in hopes of engaging a German Tiger II tank before the war in Europe ended, without success. (*Patton Museum*)

In March 1945, the Ordnance Committee authorized 1,000 examples of the Heavy Tank T26E4 as pictured here. Unlike the pilot, T24E4 rushed to the ETO that had its hydro-pneumatic equilibrator springs mounted on the roof of its turret. On production examples, the springs were incorporated into the vehicle's turret. By the war's end, only twenty-five T26E4s came out of the factory doors. (*TACOM*)

RA PD 104248A

Pictured here is a version of the Pershing armed with a 105mm howitzer that came out of the factory too late to see combat. The vehicle's designation was the Medium Tank M45. The M45 had authorized storage for seventy-four main gun rounds. A few of the M45s saw service during the Korean War. (*TACOM*)

Rivaling the German thinking embodied in their wartime Maus super-heavy tank, the Americans came up with their own super-heavy and impractical Heavy Tank T28 pictured here. It later became the 105mm GMC T95. The approximately 95-ton vehicle had a 105mm main gun. (*TACOM*)

(**Above**) Besides the T28/T95, the Ordnance Department pursued several other Heavy Tank projects in reaction to the German introduction of the Tiger II heavy tank. These included the approximately 71-ton T29 Heavy Tank pictured here. Like the T28/T95, the T29 had a 105mm main gun. Two other examples were armed with a 155mm gun and designated the T30. It appeared too late to see service in the Second World War. (*TACOM*)

(**Opposite, above**) Leaving the factory is an approximately 71-ton trackless T30E1 Heavy Tank armed with a 155mm gun. The parts of the main gun rounds had to be separately loaded, as one type of HE round weighed 95lb and another 135lb. Rate of fire was two rounds per minute. The vehicle's gun shield had a maximum thickness of 279mm (11in). (*TACOM*)

(**Opposite, below**) Unlike the T29 that received power from a liquid-cooled gasoline powered engine, the T30 got an air-cooled gasoline engine, seen here, labeled as the AV-1790-3. It developed 810 gross hp at 2,800rpms and provided the tank a top speed on level roads of 22mph. (*TACOM*)

Bibliography

Baily, Charles, *Faint Praise: American Tanks and Tank Destroyers during World War II* (Hamden, CT: Archon, 1983).

Estes, Kenneth, *Marines Under Armor: The Marine Corps and the Armored Fighting Vehicle, 1916–2000* (Annapolis, Md.: Naval Institute Press, 2000).

Gabel, Dr Christopher R., *Seek, Strike and Destroy: US Army Tank Destroyer Doctrine in World War II* (Fort Leavenworth, Kansas: US Army Command and General Staff College, 1985).

Hunnicutt, R.P., *Sherman: A History of the American Medium Tank* (Taurus Enterprises: 1978).

Hunnicutt, R.P., *Firepower: A History of the American Heavy Tank* (Novato, CA: Presidio, 1998).

Hunnicutt, R.P., *Pershing: A History of the Medium Tank T20 Series* (Bellingham, WA: Feist, 1971).

Hunnicutt, R.P., *Half-Track: A History of American Semi-Tracked Vehicles* (Novato, CA: Presidio, 2001).

Hunnicutt, R.P., *Stuart: A History of the American Light Tank* (Novato, CA: Presidio, 1992).

Johnson, David E., *Fast Tanks and Heavy Bombers: Innovation in the US Army, 1917–1945* (Ithaca, NY: Cornell University Press, 1998).

Mayo, Lida, *The Ordnance Department: On Beachhead and Battlefront*, United States Army in World War II (Washington D.C.: Office of the Chief of Military History, United States Army, 1968).

Thomson, Harry C. and Mayo, Lida, *The Ordnance Department: Procurement and Supply* (Washington: Office of the Chief of Military History, US Army, 1960).

Yeide, Harry, *The Tank Killers: A History of America's World War II Tank Destroyer Force* (PA: Casemate, 2004).

Yeide, Harry, *The Infantry's Armor: The US Army's Separate Tank Battalions in World War II* (PA: Stackpole Books, 2010).